APPLES OF THE MUMMY'S EYE:
The Dickerson Sisters

Mummy Range   *Photo by Alan Dakan, late 30s.*

By Elyse Deffke Bliss
in collaboration with
Alice Cora Dickerson

Frontispiece: The cover of this book is a collage print made by Alice Dickerson July, 1993. It depicts Alice and Helen helping clear their homesteaded land, as described on pages i and 17.

This book is dedicated to all
those who sort of knew the Dickerson Sisters,
and for
those who knew them better and therefore loved them,
and for
those who didn't know them at all but wish they had
because they had always heard of them,
and for
those who want to know of pioneers who did live,
though meagerly, lifelong on a western homestead.
—Elyse Bliss

My gratitude to Tom Canfield, whose drawings are, as always, a delight; to Mike Wittmer, for his excellent computer work; to Mary Ellen Johnston, Ann Gouin and Normajean Bartel for their constructive criticism; posthumously to Mrs. Gertrude Spaulding for being Greeley High School's most famous and beloved senior English teacher, at least to Mary Ellen, Normajean and Elyse; to Barbara Jean Foster Davis, Sue Stephens, Barbara Hyde and Reverend and Mrs. Vic Urban, John Slay U.S.F.S. and U.S.F.S. Estes-Poudre District Ranger Mike Lloyd for their assistance; and last, but not least, to my husband, Charles W. Bliss, for his patience over an extended period of time while this book was being written.

—Elyse Deffke Bliss

In addition, honorable mention to a young man, Fred Lesnick, who faithfully visits Alice daily after work to make certain she is all right. And to his parents, who must have somehow, some time instilled this unique quality in him.

Text and poetry by Elyse Deffke Bliss
Text in collaboration with
Alice C. Dickerson

Drawings by Tom Canfield

Cover painting by Alice C. Dickerson

Typesetting, cover graphic & maps by
M.D. Wittmer

Printed by Johnson Printing

Contents

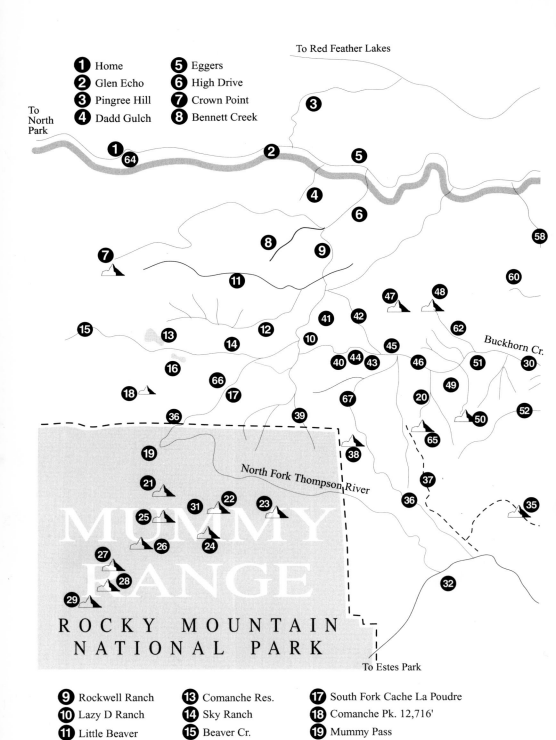

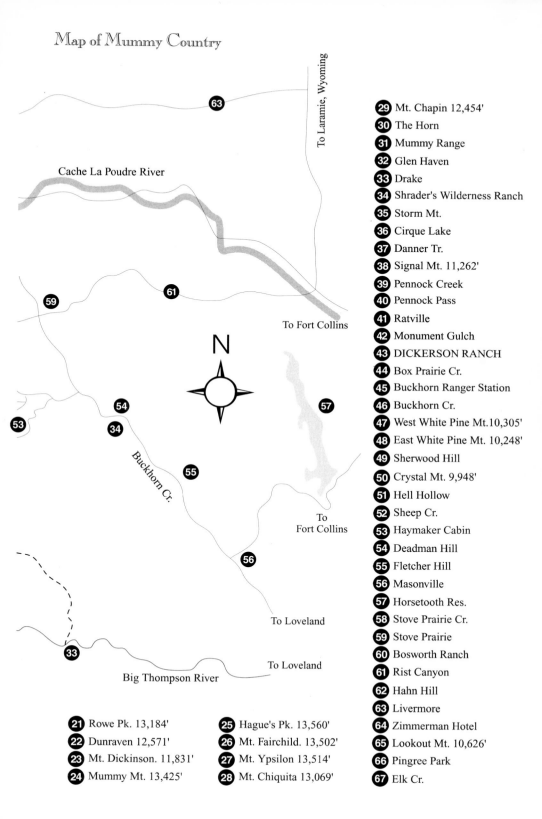

Map of Mummy Country

To Laramie, Wyoming

63

Cache La Poudre River

61

59

To Fort Collins

N

54

53

34

57

Buckhorn Cr.

55

To Fort Collins

56

To Loveland

33

To Loveland

Big Thompson River

29 Mt. Chapin 12,454'
30 The Horn
31 Mummy Range
32 Glen Haven
33 Drake
34 Shrader's Wilderness Ranch
35 Storm Mt.
36 Cirque Lake
37 Danner Tr.
38 Signal Mt. 11,262'
39 Pennock Creek
40 Pennock Pass
41 Ratville
42 Monument Gulch
43 DICKERSON RANCH
44 Box Prairie Cr.
45 Buckhorn Ranger Station
46 Buckhorn Cr.
47 West White Pine Mt. 10,305'
48 East White Pine Mt. 10,248'
49 Sherwood Hill
50 Crystal Mt. 9,948'
51 Hell Hollow
52 Sheep Cr.
53 Haymaker Cabin
54 Deadman Hill
55 Fletcher Hill
56 Masonville
57 Horsetooth Res.
58 Stove Prairie Cr.
59 Stove Prairie
60 Bosworth Ranch
61 Rist Canyon
62 Hahn Hill
63 Livermore
64 Zimmerman Hotel
65 Lookout Mt. 10,626'
66 Pingree Park
67 Elk Cr.

21 Rowe Pk. 13,184'
22 Dunraven 12,571'
23 Mt. Dickinson. 11,831'
24 Mummy Mt. 13,425'

25 Hague's Pk. 13,560'
26 Mt. Fairchild. 13,502'
27 Mt. Ypsilon 13,514'
28 Mt. Chiquita 13,069'

PREFACE

Along the Front Range of the Colorado Rockies are nine mountain chains running from north to south. If one could stand on the eastern Colorado border with wide angle vision and, unobstructed by fog, smog or a natural earth curvature barrier look to the west, the chains of peaks would appear as unending miles of a craggy lower border of a big Colorado sky. Seeing this, one would sense that these magnificent peaks characterize Colorado and that, if one knows anything at all about the origins of Earth's waterways, he would know that from those summits the lifeblood of many rivers begins. And he would know that from those rivers vegetation is nurtured that provides the sustenance of human and animal life, not only to Colorado, but to many states through which their waters flow.

Mummy Range.   *Photo by Alice Dickerson, 1980.*

One of the chains lying toward the northern end of the magnificent panoramic vista is called, oddly, the Mummy Range.

In contrast to the rounded, smooth western slope of the range, the eastern portion is dotted with deep cirques, formed by ice chiseling rock, the ice finally vanishing and leaving in its

CHAPIN 12,454 CHIQUITA 13,069 YPSILON 13,514 FAIRCHILD 13,502 MUMMY 13,425 HAGUES 13,560 DUNRAVEN 12,570

Mummy Range, looking west from 2 mi. north of Loveland exit on I-25.

wake a telltale depression. But the range was not named by an Egyptian, at least no one thinks so, but rather by someone, possibly Albert Bierstadt in the 1870s, whose imagination pictured the skyline as resembling a mummy lying on its back. Hague's Peak, 13,560', the range's highest, is the Mummy's head; Mount Fairchild, 13,502', forms drawn-up knees; Mt. Ypsilon, 13,514', with its ice-carved "Y", represents the Mummy's feet; Mt. Chapin, 12,454', and Mt. Chiquita, 13,069', are footstools. But there are more theories on how that mummy is lying. Alice Dickerson, for example, described it as seen from east of Pingree Park looking west. Others see it differently. Alice has the advantage herein, however; this is her book, so her view is pictured.

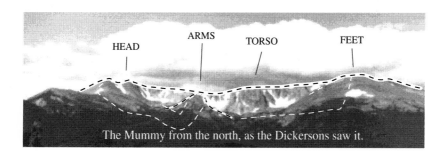

HEAD ARMS TORSO FEET

The Mummy from the north, as the Dickersons saw it.

The Arapaho Indians perhaps were more realistic, calling the range "White Owls" for the white snowfields dotting the mountainsides like fresh molted feathers. A diplomat probably would call it "The Mummy Upon Which A Couple Of White Owls Shed Their Feathers" to please everyone.

The southernmost peaks of the Mummy Range are in Rocky Mountain National Park and the northern range is within Roosevelt National Forest, Comanche Peaks Wilderness Area and is south-west of Pingree Park, the mountain summer campus of Colorado State University.

The Cache la Poudre South Fork, known as the "Little South",

12

trickles down from the Mummy Range, which separates it from the North Fork of the Big Thompson River.

The Mummy rises above all the lower lands around it, as a woman spreading her skirt evenly flat in the wind. Under this skirt, to the south and east of the range, in 1911, horse thieves were gathering their four-footed loot and trailing them from Estes Park, across somewhere near Stormy Peaks and to a secret hiding place up in a deep canyon, Pennock Creek, they say, where a log cabin and pole corral had been built. From there they trailed them, probably at night to avoid detection, to North Park.

Below the western portion of the Mummy's skirt, Lulu City and surrounding country were mostly deserted except for a few diehard prospectors.

To the north, the Cache la Poudre Canyon was the scene of several cattle ranches and of much talk and work about dams, ditches and irrigation for the farmers out on the plains. And, to the east and northeast of the range, some homesteaders were cutting out an existence by hauling poles and posts to farmers on the eastern plains. Others, like those on the Poudre, were running cattle and still others were, like those west of the Mummy, still doggedly prospecting, hoping to strike a lucky vein and make their fortune.

Pennock Pass, northeast of the Mummy, had been hewn out of the woods some years earlier, a narrow, straight-up, straight-down trail for horses and livestock. East of the pass was the Buckhorn Canyon, nestled and twisted down between cliffs and mountains, leading to Masonville and hence to the plains below.

No road buddied up to the little Buckhorn stream in those early days; wagons etched their tracks over mountaintops, up hills and down into valleys.

Along the Buckhorn drainage were several early homesteads. In particular, those nearest the uppermost valley through which Box Prairie Creek flowed, nestled on the east against Pennock Mountain were, in order of their descent down the Buckhorn: (1)**Oat Osbern**, between the valley and the ranger station; (2)**Mack Hammond**, below the United States Forest Service ranger station; (3)**Tom Blair**, on White Pine; (4)**Ralph Derby** on Buckhorn Creek (a rascal); (5)**Ed Sherwood**, on Cascade Creek; (6)**Mr. Ballard**, on Elk Creek; (7)**Mr. Lakey**, near "the Horn" on Buckhorn Creek; (8)**Belle Morrison**, Hell Hollow Creek near Burkharts, about 4 or 5 miles below Box Prairie Valley; (9)**Gooch**, a few miles above Crystal Mountain Road; (10)**Elizabeth Geiger**,

C

in Deadman Canyon; (11)**Charley Mason**, down in the valley toward Masonville, which was named for his parents; (12)**Wess Roswell** on Crystal Mountain; he built the stake and rider fence from Estes Park to the Poudre, presumably to divide livestock pastures; remnants of the fence are still visible by the ranger station, Dickersons', Pennock Pass, Pingree Park and other scattered places. The fence remnants should be preserved for historic records as it was a fantastic feat building such a fence, especially

Stake and Rider fence remnant.   Photo by Elyse Bliss, 1993.

John Turner homestead barn.   Photo by Miriam Mohr

for that distance and in the mountains; (13)**Latman**, (14)**Heinz** (15)**Gene and Ed Smith** and (16)**John Turner** all lived on Crystal Mountain.

To the north of the little Box Prairie Valley, in Monument Gulch, lived **Will Gard** and **George Goodson**.

d

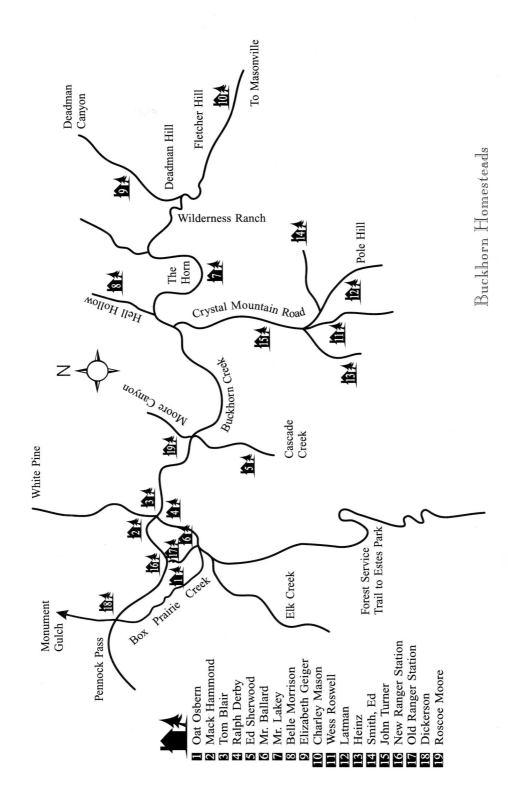

Buckhorn Homesteads

White Pine

Deadman Canyon

Deadman Hill

Fletcher Hill

To Masonville

10

9

Wilderness Ranch

The Horn

14

Hell Hollow

8

7

Pole Hill

Crystal Mountain Road

12

N

Moore Canyon

15

11

Buckhorn Creek

13

Cascade Creek

9

5

Monument Gulch

Pennock Pass

2

3

4

6

White Pine

16

1 17

18

Box   Prairie   Creek

Elk Creek

Forest Service
Trail to Estes Park

1 Oat Osbern
2 Mack Hammond
3 Tom Blair
4 Ralph Derby
5 Ed Sherwood
6 Mr. Ballard
7 Mr. Lakey
8 Belle Morrison
9 Elizabeth Geiger
10 Charley Mason
11 Wess Roswell
12 Latman
13 Heinz
14 Smith, Ed
15 John Turner
16 New Ranger Station
17 Old Ranger Station
18 Dickerson
19 Roscoe Moore

Across Pennock Pass into the Little South Poudre valley, homesteaders were **Dave Barnes**, who donated a 40-acre wheat field to the railroad to start the town of Loveland and had a Monument Gulch hill named for him; **Dave Quigley**, just below his uncle, Dave Barnes, now the Rockwell Ranch owned by Ft. Collins and Greeley Water Supply; **Hugh Ramsey**, Frank Koenig's father-in-law, the first homesteader of Colorado State University's Pingree Park; **John Derby**, on what is now the Lazy D Ranch; **Tom Bennett** was the early homesteader on Beaver Creek, now the Sky Camp of the Lutheran Church (winter 1909-1910 he occupied a cabin on Will Gard's homestead in Monument Gulch; it was so heavily infested with packrats that both Gard and Bennett called it "Ratville"; the cabin is gone, but the name stuck; Bennett Creek and Campground are named for him).

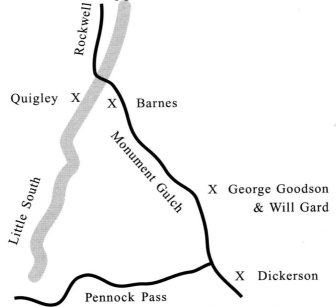

To the south of the Box Prairie Valley a trail accommodated foot travelers from the Buckhorn Ranger Station to Estes Park.

The aspen-filled Box Prairie Valley veered gradually downward to drain into the Buckhorn Creek. Quakie (aspen) leaves whispering in gentle breezes and ever-so-soft rippling sounds of the creek encouraged a 1911 passerby to stop and just listen. An old soddy blended into the eastern hillside of the little valley, its doorway grown over with undisturbed grasses and tall aspen shoots—proof that man, though once there, no longer inhabited the place.

ſ

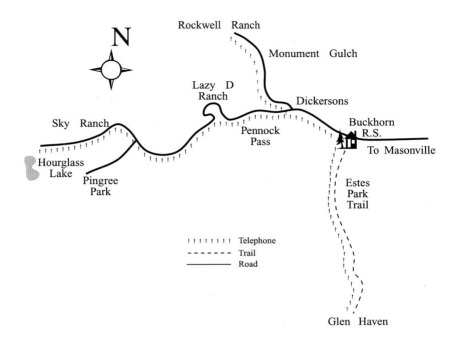

Rockwell Ranch

Monument Gulch

Lazy D
Ranch

Dickersons

Sky Ranch

Buckhorn
R.S.

Pennock
Pass

To Masonville

Hourglass
Lake

Pingree
Park

Estes
Park
Trail

↑↑↑↑↑↑↑ Telephone
- - - - - - Trail
———— Road

Glen Haven

Later the unmistakable sounds of chains in motion against wooden doubletrees, the casual, almost contented, sneezing of something equine and the creaking of wagon wheels as they rolled through uneven and rocky mountain soil interrupted the quiet murmurings of peaceful aspen and rivulets. The Sam Dickersons had arrived in Mummy Country. From that time forward the Box Prairie Valley would be known as the Dickerson Ranch.

"We had a wagon much like this."....Alice Dickerson.

g

INTRODUCTION

Try to visualize a wagon trail high in the Buckhorn Canyon bordered by acres of aspen and patches of willows. Imagine wood smoke curling into your nostrils. Pretend to hear Steller's jays squawking from within the forest and the incessant chattering of chickarees as they scold wielders of double-bitted axes methodically chopping at aspen trees and echoing throughout the valley. The axe sounds must seem quite foreign to the wildlife inhabitants. Probably even more alien to the forest creatures would be a crosscut saw cutting rasping sounds into the crisp morning mountain air.

Fascinating to today's passerby if he could regress in time would be the sight of a very gentle, relaxed horse at the end of a long pole, walking round and round. On closer examination he could spot a cable somehow pulling stumps from the ground, roots and all, as the horse circles. But the most fascinating part of the entire scene would be the tiny little girl in her quaint home-fashioned dress leading the horse.

He could direct his attention toward where the menfolks are sawing and chopping. Another almost-as-tiny little girl dressed similarly to the other would catch his eye. She would be dragging trash sticks as big as she could handle and stacking them for the grownups to burn when the time was right.

He could visualize a small sod-roofed cabin and a short, ample, old-country-looking woman emerging from the doorway carrying a dishpan from which she would heave the morning's dishwater a good distance through the air.

It is how the scene must have looked as Sam Dickerson's three-generation family were "proving up" their half-homestead, reportedly one of the last issued in the State of Colorado. It was 1914. Leading the horse around and around was 4½-year-old Helen Dickerson; picking up sticks was Alice, Helen's 6-year-old big sister. Helen loved horses and was proud to be helping her family in such a grownup way...and it was fun, too.

I
BEGATS
Pre-1774-1911

Begats

Begats are confusing and sometimes amusing
When studied with discerning eye;
Dickersons were perfection in that direction—
Juniors and namesakes didn't die.
Cora's grandpa great great was also Sam's great
From Old Josh and Susannah's decree;
Both were descended though distance defended—
They were limbs off the same family tree.

Old Joshua and Susannah Dickerson begat Thomas, Joshua, Eli, John, William, Levi and a covey of eight girls.

Now William married Elizabeth Doney and begat James, Tom, Eli, William and probably some girls. This William, Junior, known as "Big Bill", married Rebecca Eaton and they begat Sam, Isaac, Kins, Emma, Sade, Alva, Levi, Amanda, Hannah, Lib, Adda and Myrtle, who were twins. The only one of this lot pertinent to this particular story is Sam, whose full name was Samuel Doney Dickerson, born July 4, 1853.

Now to confuse the reader a bit, let's go back to that covey of eight girls begat by Old Josh and Suzie. One daughter from that covey was Rebecca Dickerson, born in 1774. She met David Howard, nine years older than she, and married him in 1794. These two begat some mini-Howards, those being Alice in 1795, Susannah in 1797, James in 1799, Mary in 1803, Rachel in 1807, Joshua D in 1812 (remember him) and Rebecca in 1815.

Little Josh didn't hang around home long. Everybody thought his mom, Rebecca, was going to die, so Uncle Eli Dickerson's wife, Polly, took Josh home to live with them. After all, Eli was the only Dickerson son who had no children, so it seemed logical. As it turned out, Rebecca didn't die, but Eli and Polly kept J.D. anyway. Becky and Dave probably didn't miss him as they had their hands full.

Well, when Joshua D. Howard grew up, he and Harriet Warfel tied the knot in 1834 and begat David A. in 1835, George W. in 1837 and Susan R. in 1845. One wonders why he didn't name one after Eli. Wallace B. Layport, apparently an orphan born in 1854, joined these Howards when he was a lad of 12 or 13. These were Civil War times and George died the first day of 1863 in the Battle of Stone River, Tennessee.

David also died young, cause unknown, in 1857, but not until after he married Belinda J. Ross in 1854 and begat a child, Cora Emma Howard April 30, 1858, born after his untimely early death.

Remember Sam Doney Dickerson a few paragraphs up? He and Cora Emma Howard were married September 26, 1878.

Sam Doney Dickerson
1878   *Cora Emma Howard*
1879

They begat Earl Ross Dickerson September 19, 1879, William Ray Dickerson April 2, 1887 and Allen Dwight Dickerson April 4, 1897.

* * * * * * * * * * * * * * *

Meanwhile, in Williamsburg, Ohio, another family important to this story had begun. Somebody begat William Henry Foster in 1857, Theophilus Gaines Foster in 1855, and Tom, Mary and Suzie. Theophilus became owner of Foster's Department Store, mayor, bank president, Chairman of the Board of the local furniture factory and superintendent of the Presbyterian Sunday School. Tom was a doctor in Washington, D.C. during World War I, Mary married Lake Peterson, Suzie married George Hagemann and George and Henry (Bill) became farmer/rancher types.

William Henry Foster married Sarah Peterson, who was born in 1863, and they begat Edwin, Theophilus Gaines (T.G. for short, for obvious reasons), Alice, Stella (born July 12, 1884) and Elizabeth.

Henry and Sarah moved their family from Williamsburg to Washington, Kansas, because daughter Stella had a bad case of asthma. They thought in Kansas she would be able to breathe better.

*William Henry Foster, the
Dickerson sisters' maternal
grandfather. Old Foster photo.*

*Sarah Peterson, the Dickerson
sisters' maternal grandmother.
Old Foster photo.*

However, they found her not much improved, so later they sent her by prairie schooner to an aunt in Windsor, Colorado. That aunt, incidentally, had married Kins Dickerson, brother of Sam, and the plot thickens.

Stella's trip to Colorado could not have been too comfortable bouncing along the dusty prairie trail and her anguish at leaving her parents and siblings behind must have squelched any eager anticipation she may have had for entering the strange, new land. In later years, she recalled that trip to her daughters and told of prairie wolves and Indians on her westward journey.

* * * * * * * * * *

Now Sam Dickerson had also migrated to the tiny town of Eaton, Colorado from Williamsburg and Roscoe, Ohio, accompanied by his wife, Cora and their tiny son, Earl, probably in the early 1880s. Eaton was in dire need of a blacksmith, so

Stella Foster.   Old Foster photo.

Sam answered the call from his uncle, Benjamin Eaton, who even paid his way. Benjamin was Governor of Colorado from 1885 to 1887.

Ex-Governor Eaton, driver. Eaton, 1907.
Photo by Wm. Ray Dickerson.

First Eaton blacksmith shop, late 1800s. Old Dickerson photo.

Sam became the town's first blacksmith, and a good one. His other two sons were born in Eaton.

Number one son, Earl, grew up and worked with his dad in the blacksmith shop when he was around town. He was intrigued by the mountains, however, and worked on the Michigan Ditch near Cameron Pass above the Poudre Canyon one year. While there he

Earl Dickerson and Michigan Ditch gang on Cameron Pass.
Early 1900s Dickerson photo.

explored the area quite extensively and, among other things, found a petrified banana, nuts and a lemon on Specimen Mountain. He also went, just for fun, by wagon to Oregon with his aunt Sade's husband, which took almost three months. He nearly settled in Idaho because he said he had never seen anything like the big vegetables they grew there due to volcanic ash.

One can put two and two together when figuring how Stella Foster, of Windsor, and Earl Dickerson, of Eaton, met. Probably Kins and Sam, being brothers, occasionally traveled one way or the other to get caught up on brotherly things. Chances are they brought their wives and offspring and Earl's and Stella's eyes met across a crowded room. Wherever or however they met, they were married August 19, 1906 and lived in Eaton, where Earl helped his dad in the blacksmith shop and worked at odd jobs in and out of Eaton.

Brotherly visit to Windsor. L-R, sitting: Stella, Belle (Kins' wife), Kins Dickerson. L-R, standing: Earl Dickerson, Vera (Kins' daughter), 1907. Old Dickerson stereoscope photo.

Earl and Stella were very important, because they begat the two heroines of this story, Alice Cora Dickerson on June 23, 1908 and Helen Esther Dickerson on November 9, 1909.

* *

A man named Mack Hammond immigrated into Colorado from Ohio and homesteaded in the Buckhorn Canyon west of Masonville. He, the Sam Dickerson family and Stella Foster, all originally from Ohio, crossed trails and became the foundation stones of the homestead where Alice and Helen were to spend their lives being the apples of the Mummy's eye.

Alice, who had just given Helen her teddy bear and Helen, who had just thrown it on the ground. 1911. Photo by Stella Dickerson.

II
EARLY HOMESTEAD
YEARS
1911-1930

A Move to the Hills

They wound up the creek to their claim 'neath the peak
*   With all of their earthly need;*
Mules stretched and strained 'til their energy drained
*   And they certainly earned their feed.*
The old cabin reeked and its sod roof leaked,
*   But it was Dickersons' home for awhile—*
'Til they cleared some land sawing trees by hand
*   So the homestead could be proved to its file.*

One of Dickerson's best customers at his blacksmith shop was Mack Hammond, who journeyed to Eaton frequently from his Buckhorn Canyon homestead. Hauling poles and posts to Eaton farmers, he often needed blacksmithing done while he was in town. Not only did he and Sam become close friends, but he

Dickerson blacksmith shop, Eaton. Sam on right.
Early 1900s. Old Dickerson photo.

captured the adoration of Sam's little grandaughters, Alice and Helen. In fact they fondly tabbed him "Uncle Mack". He earned

the title, because in spite of the weeklong round trip with his team and wagon, he always brought the little girls a puppy, kitten, baby chick or some other special treat. He must have missed the women in his family; his wife had passed away and his daughter was a nurse overseas and became a World War I nurse in Egypt. Alice and Helen never saw Uncle Mack's daughter.

"Uncle" Mack Hammond, 1913.
Photo by Ray Dickerson.

The Dickerson families enjoyed trekking up to the Hammond place on the Buckhorn to go camping. The 4th of July had become an annual event; they traveled up in wagons for big picnic celebrations. They liked it so much up there that one day Uncle Mack came to Eaton and

4th of July picnic at Mack Hammond's, late 1800s. Sam lying sideways, his father behind him. Cora to the left of Sam. Old Dickerson photo.

announced, "There's still a half-homestead left up in the Buckhorn. If you want it, go get it. It's the last homestead left in this part of the country." Sam Dickerson filed his claim. That was in 1911. Not only did the Dickerson family like the high mountain country, but Sam had acquired an alcohol addiction. Thus his family and Hammond supported him in his decision to move, hoping he would be far enough away from the source of his addiction to achieve a cure through abstinence.

Sam pouring a drink. About 1910.   Old Dickerson photo.

So away they went, lock, stock and barrel. With wagon loaded and pulled by two mules and two horses, seven Dickersons descended upon their newly-claimed soil from the sovereign State of Colorado.

The Homestead Act of 1862 was a law enacted by Congress May 20, 1862 under President Abraham Lincoln for the purpose of getting public domain into private ownership. The law provided that any citizen might, upon payment of the nominal fee of $5 or $10, enter upon and hold any unappropriated quarter section of the public lands valued at $1.25 per acre or any one-eighth section valued at $2.50 per acre, and after 5 years' residence become the sole owner. This law proved of great value in settling the lands of the West. But the law had failed in Colorado's arid climate, because the size of the homestead could not be made to fit the variety of growing conditions west of the 100th Meridian. Thus Sam Dickerson had his work cut out for him; the land he was

Dickerson family on Lower Buckhorn, early 1900s.
Old Dickerson stereoscope photo.

homesteading was climatically harsh and it would be a difficult task to create a living for himself and his wife, let alone two more generations to follow.

Sam and Cora, Earl and Stella with their young daughters Alice and Helen and Earl's youngest brother Allen moved their earthly goods into an old abandoned sod-roofed log cabin on the property. A man named Lytle had built the tiny building, located below where the present Dickerson house stands, some years

before. The peak west of this location was named for Mr. Lytle. The first summer and fall they camped in the old cabin. The sod roof leaked like a sieve, so they covered the beds inside with tarps. The soddy was constructed with poles very close together and had sagebrush growing from its roof, so it was just a step better than living under the stars. Outside they employed a "great big bumbershoot" (umbrella) above the table. The bumbershoot also was used frequently over the buggy when family members went up and down the Buckhorn.

Dickerson stereoscope photo showing bumbershoot. Allen and his mother Cora, camped by Haymaker Cabin about 1908, before homestead.

While living in the soddy the first few months they were plagued with packrats joining them within the holey walls. One day 12-year-old gunman Allen, coming upon a pesky rat getting into food and running along the log walls, shot it. Proudly he posed outside the cabin holding his ratty trophy for his picture to be taken.

Allen with ratty trophy.   Old Dickerson photo, 1911.

As soon as they could get organized, Sam, Cora and Allen moved across the valley into tents so they could be near their building site.

In the late fall Stella and the girls were left at the Lytle cabin while the rest of the family had gone to Eaton. One afternoon the girls and their dogs were playing in the yard when a spring wagonload of men came up the road shooting their high-powered rifles while yelling atop rearing and plunging horses. By the time Stella had collected the girls and their now-panicked canine friends into the cabin, the men had stopped out in front demanding they come out. Stella waited inside with pistol in hand, but they did not attempt to come in and soon rode off. They were going hunting over Pennock Pass to the Rockwell Ranch and were quite inebriated. Stella was relieved when the rest of the family returned.

Quickly the men built a food storage cellar and cleared enough land to grow a garden. The original cellar was outdoors and had a dirt roof. In later years, Alice did not remember if it ever froze inside.

"If it got that cold," she said, "I suspect they put a bucket of hot coals in there to prevent the vegetables from freezing."

Needing to "prove up" on their homestead, they were required to work every year for five years building fences, houses and growing a garden so they would not have to pay.

Before the large-scale forest clearing began, a mountain lion

Original cellar. Grandma Cora and son Allen.
Old Dickerson photo, 1911.

was spotted in the willows alongside the road close to the soddy. One of the non-resident relatives was preparing to heave a rock at it, which unnerved the Forest Ranger who had happened by. He said, as he loped up the road away from the cat, "Wait 'til I get out of here before you throw your rock!"

That ranger, Joe Ryan, did not want to stick around much anyway. His favorite pastime was maintaining the Estes Park Trail telephone line, the first in the area, which followed a nice 4'-wide trail with well-built bridges from the Buckhorn Ranger Station to Drake, in the Big Thompson Canyon. He used horses in summer and snowshoes during the winter. But after he married the object of this pastime, the Estes Park Central telephone operator, he suddenly lost interest in checking the line to Estes Park and it soon fell into disrepair. All he wanted was to stay home.

Ranger maintaining telephone line.

The first order of business, after completing the cellar and the first portion of the big house so the family could keep warm and dry, was to clear more land. It was a formidable task; aspen trees, willows and some pine occupied proposed meadow sites.

16

Knowing that lodgepole land was not good for crops due to its acidic soil and too many rocks, they decided aspen would be the best for plowing and planting oats for the horses and a big potato patch for the family. The land clearing was begun with urgency, because they were having to haul hay up to feed the horses. Thus for economic reasons they needed to get feed planted and harvested.

For the next few years the Dickersons worked hard to fill the requirements. They cleared and fenced enough land so adequate food could be raised. Helen described the land-clearing procedure: "The trees were all cut with ax and hand saws. The stumps were left two feet or more high to leave room to tie a cable to; this was fastened to a cylinder that tightened as the horse went round and round at the end of a long pole. This pulled the long roots out with the stumps making the ground so it could be plowed. I led the horse to pull the stumps. It was a very gentle horse and I was age 4½ when I started helping. All the trash had to be piled and burned. Alice and I drug the small sticks we could handle and the grownups put them into the fire. We weren't allowed too close to the fire."

The seven Dickersons worked together as a family preparing their homestead to become a home. Alice and Helen, who as little girls made play out of their work, fondly recalled, "When the day was done there wasn't a better place than Grandma's feather bed."

* * * * * * * * *

Dickerson land-clearing machinery - Alice said:

"Pop used to plow sod for planting grain & hay."

"Pop used a disc like this to break up sod."

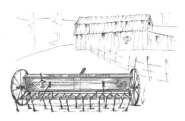

"He used this kind of harrow after plowing field."

"Pop used a seeder like this one to sow grain."

For about a year all seven of the newly-established mountain family lived in the first house built, which was certainly better than the airy little soddy. Then another house was built across the newly-cleared meadow because the back of the first house col-

Original Earl Dickerson cabin.   Old Dickerson photo, 1912.

lected water and it aggravated Stella's asthma. In addition, the original house was situated in the shade and snow clung to the aprons around it all winter, making it difficult for the little girls to play outside. The new site was sunny and the wind blew the snow away more readily than at the original site, which was shady and protected from the wind.

The brand new little log cabin was the home where Alice and Helen were to live the rest of their lives.

Aunt Alice (Stella's sister) fishing on Buckhorn Creek near Crystal Mountain turnoff, early 1900s. Dickerson stereoscope.

Poles and Posts

Settlers hauled posts and poles to the souls
   In Eaton, a long way at best;
With team-wagon skills they traveled the hills
   Camping at night for a rest;
Sometimes it was cold and quilts were unrolled
   To wrap Helen and Alice up snug;
Hot rocks wrapped neat helped warm tiny feet
   They'd ride snug as bugs in a rug.

After clearing enough land and building adequate structures for immediate needs, the family anxiously set about the task of earning a living. Most of the early Buckhorn homesteaders made a living at one time or another hauling poles and posts and the Dickersons were no exception; timber was their first money-making venture on the homestead.

They had two teams; one of horses, the other of mules. When hauling to town, they usually took two loads. In the early days they had to travel up two long hills, Sherwood and Deadman, which were no longer used after the Buckhorn Canyon road was built. When the wagons, heavily loaded, started up one of these steep inclines, Sam and Earl took one team off its wagon and tacked it on to the other wagon's team to help pull up the load. Then they took the teams back down to the other wagon and used them both to labor up the hill.

The posts acquired by the homesteaders were in much demand. Mostly Ponderosa hearts, they were the standing charred forest leavings called pitch. Not all Ponderosa pine trees contain pitch, a non-white marble-looking substance that gets oozy in the hot sun. The posts were split by wedges and sledge hammers; then the soft wood and char were hewn with an axe. Even little Alice fixed some posts and sold them herself for twenty cents apiece. Pitch posts last a long time without artificial treating; thus the desirability to fence-builders everywhere. Dickersons used a few of the posts for their own fences, some of which are still there, but most of the good pitch posts they sold.

Pole wagons were expertly prepared for the extremely heavy loads, many which were horse-drawn all the way to Eaton and over some of the most primitive roads imaginable. Four long stakes were secured into rings on the front and back of each side of the wagon, to keep the poles from rolling off. After the poles were stacked to horse carrying capacity, heavy log chains were used to hold the load tightly secured in place. On top of this load were secured a "grub-box" containing food, heavy quilts rolled in canvas, a bag of grain and hay for the horses. When going downhill with a heavy load, a wagon had to be held back by brakes made with wooden blocks secured into iron clamps, which were fastened to a hardwood bar under the wagon. The brake rope was held in one hand and the team reins in the other.

In cold weather the men often walked when driving the team to keep from freezing; sometimes they walked almost all the way. If Alice and Helen were along and it was really cold, rocks heated on a campfire were wrapped and placed at their feet and they snuggled in a quilt wrapped around them.

"Keep me from crying, mostly," recalled Helen. "My feet would get so cold, I could hardly stand it. Pop would get the rock warm and pull the quilt down over it and my feet." Horses and mules had to be fed and rested morning, noon and night due to the long and strenuous journey. At noon the family stopped, built a campfire when possible, and ate a hot lunch while the horses ate and rested. As Alice put it, "The 'gas engine' didn't work so well without food on the front end; you had to feed your car."

If the weather was good, they put up a tent and stayed all night, making certain the animals received plenty of food, water and rest. Sometimes they stayed in the cabin at the old Haymaker place at Sheep Creek. The cabin was preferred instead of a tent because of the abundance of rattlesnakes. Other times they stayed the night in a barn at Masonville, all, of course, depending on the weather, load size or any other variable that could occur.

The Masonville barn, where they frequently stayed, had an aisle with hay in it, upon which the family rolled out their bedrolls. The horses ate across the aisle. The bedrolls, which Stella made, were heavy quilts made with cotton batting, almost like mattresses. Those nights on the hay listening to the soft munching of the grateful resting horses were not without

Earl cooking lunch over an open fire.
Dickerson stereoscopic photo, 1913.

disadvantages. One night Helen, 2 or 3 years old, kept frantically motioning toward her ear. Her mother, seeing some blood on the ear, pulled out a "stinkbug" with tweezers.

"Our grub box was not the choicest of food when you didn't have much money to buy things with. Bread. Beans. Not much. Potatoes, maybe. We had to have water for the horses, so we camped by the Buckhorn," Alice recalled.

One night, while the family was all in a row sleeping on a tarpaulin on the floor in the Sheep Creek cabin, Grandpa Sam leaped up, obviously alarmed. Everyone reacted instantly, saw a fire and quickly doused it with water while Grandpa still hopped around on one leg trying to get his pants on.

Other occasional stopover camping spots were Stella Burkhart's place about four or five miles below Dickersons'; Shraders', near what is now Wilderness Ranch; and Langstons. Reportedly Burkharts' on Crystal Mountain was the highest altitude a rattlesnake had ever been reported in the Buckhorn country.

One of Dickersons' favorite camp spots was right in the middle of what is now Horsetooth Reservoir, near where the old Stout Post Office was, in a rock house. Alice said, "The schoolhouse is gone. I don't know why they didn't take the windows out of the schoolhouse instead of tearing it down; let the fish swim in and out. They left it 'til the last thing; it was rock. When the water goes down, you can see the rubble and pinnacle they left."

Geary home in Stout across from Stout Post Office (now under Horsetooth Reservoir) where Dickersons stayed occasionally. Dickerson photo collection.

The Buckhorn Canyon road as modern folks know it, is a relatively new rendition. The early road (1800s) to Pingree Park, Lazy D Ranch, Gards and the Rockwell Ranch went over Pole Hill, Crystal Mountain and Sherwood Hill. Ranger Helmick, Earl and Allen Dickerson surveyed for the first road from Moore's house through Moore Canyon to Crystal Mountain. It was built by hand and with horses, but was too low and it washed out in about three years. No road was all the way through the Buckhorn and for many years after the Dickersons arrived the road did not follow the creek closely and it consisted of many steep little hills.

When roads were icy, or anticipated to be so, the teams were shod with metal corks in their shoes to keep them and their load from sliding down a slippery hill. Uncle Mack Hammond lost a load of furniture on the icy road. The wagon slid over the bank up on top of "the Horn" and away it all went. For years a glance up the cliff brought laughs, shock or surprise at chairs, bedsteads and other household things lodged precariously in, on and around the rocks.

Cora and Earl Dickerson on lower Buckhorn Road, 1907.
Old Dickerson photo.

Hammond, while transporting a load down the Buckhorn, was rudely told once by an impatient traveler to "get out of the road." He obliged and got his wagon off, but somehow his poles stuck out the back so far the people still could not get by. Mack casually unhitched the horses and said, "there you are," and took his horses to get a drink.

Originally on the canyon road there were 21 creek crossings, but no bridges; the creek had to be forded. One advantage was that it was a convenient way for horses to get a drink.

"But," Alice remembered, "Sometimes when the water was deep, it was scary...the wagon would almost float."

After bridges were built, the road was maintained quite a few years by a team of two horses pulling a drag. Later the horses pulled a real grader, with Floyd Mason doing the work from Crystal Mountain to Horsetooth and the Big Thompson. Dickersons usually boarded the grader men when they were working near their place. One bridge was made of logs wedged between two big rock ledges. Holes were drilled in the rocks so metal pins could hold the logs. They said it would never wash out, and they were right; it is buried under driftwood and rock that was blasted when the 2nd road was built...but it is still there.

The journey to and from Eaton, about 63 miles, toting poles and posts usually took about a week. After selling the timber, for which they almost always had a market, the family bought supplies. Helen said, "Some meat, though not very much. Mostly

24

beans, salt side and flour. Almost everything else we raised in a big garden every year."

The Dickersons sold farmers timbers for hay stackers and poles for making potato dugouts. Several times they took big

Very early dugout, early 1900s.   Old Dickerson photo.

timbers down to the girls' uncle in Windsor, who had a big dugout. It was difficult to persuade mules to go head first into the dugouts, so they had to back them in. Farmers put huge crops of potatoes in dugouts during winter, so they needed a large supply of timbers. Potatoes could be held in a dugout's cold storage as long as ten months. Round posts as well as more expensive sawed timbers were used in the construction. Poles often were used as rafters, placed four inches apart. The dugouts were covered with woven wire, straw and dirt and lasted only about 10 years; then another was built.

It was, in 1917, according to the Colorado Agricultural College Extension Service in Fort Collins, *"the patriotic duty of every grower at this time to conserve every part of his crop. The great annual waste in food due to insufficient storage is a serious loss, and especially so at this time when a shortage of food exists in some countries. Tenants who feel that they are unable to construct a storage for their crops should appeal to their land owners. A storage well constructed is a permanent improvement and is indispensable to the successful marketing of the potato and apple crops."* Thus the mountain post & pole folks were providing an important resource to the fine farmers on the eastern plains.

When in Eaton, the men would talk around and find out if any of the farmers needed timber. Sometimes the farmers would go up to the Dickersons, see about stacker poles or posts, quickly inquire about cost, whether or not they would deliver and then spend the rest of the time fishing.

First Eaton blacksmith shop, late 1800s. Photo by W.R. Dickerson.

The road through the Dickerson homestead originally came through a swamp. Most roads were originally laid out following settlers' paths from cabin to cabin, with no attention given to general topography, drainage or road materials. This road was no exception. In spring the teams and wagons became mired in the mud so it took the better part of a day to get out. Mr. Sherwood one day sank his horse to its belly, and buggy to its bed. The men pried both the horse and buggy out with long poles. This inspired the Dickersons to construct a pole corduroy road there, which was used until the present dirt road was built. A "corduroy road" is one in which logs are arranged in a row over mud, then the other way on top, fastened so they will not separate and for the purpose of going over swamps without sinking.

One of the post and pole load drivers, Orr Rockwell, came over Monument Gulch with his team and wagon one day and stopped to see if Dickersons had any outgoing mail, which he would kindly transport to the nearest post office. Little Alice and Helen kept giggling and peering under the trailing ends of the poles on his wagon. Finally they told him there was a pig under there. He had no idea his pet pig had followed him. He caught it and Dickersons kept it until he returned from town.

Rockwell bought cattle in the spring and sold them in the fall. One year he had just received 100 head from southern Texas. A late May snowstorm hit and was so deep he could not feed, so he lost most of his herd. He skinned them all, took the hides to town in one wagon load and said, "This is my profit for the year." He lost two herds while he lived there and sold his place to Ft. Collins & Greeley Water Works after the 1923 flood.

When the first telephone line was completed in 1912 or 1913 from the ranger station, past Dickersons' to the Rockwell Ranch, Ranger Walt Brown took over maintaining it from Joe Ryan who, with his wife, was no longer there. Orr Rockwell, tickled to have a telephone, immediately tried it out. He called Brown and told him there was a fire ... Brown did not wait for Orr to tell him the fire was in his cookstove, so hung up and hurried out to saddle his horse and race to the fire.

Called a spur, the Estes Park line was extended, connected behind Dickersons and run through Monument Gulch. It went directly to the Rockwell Ranch; there was no road at that time south to Derbys', nor north to the Poudre Canyon.

The Children

"Today you can play", said their mama one day-
The girls squealed with delight at the thought.
They climbed up the hills and took several spills
And played with a calf they had caught.
They ran through the fields, their dog at their heels
Then decided to see Uncle Mack;
It's the bread they were lovin' fresh out of the oven
And he gave them their Sunday snack.

Because there were seldom any other children around, little Alice and Helen entertained each other or made their own fun with whatever was available, even at a very young age. Sometimes, in later years, cousins came up from Denver or Eaton, but only in the summers. Sam could hardly wait; he went to Eaton to get his other grandchildren the minute school was out. On these occasions a favorite pastime for the children was to go the mile down to the Buckhorn Ranger Station and climb all over the rocks or to the mountaintops. Later on, during their home schooling years, "town kids" came up, but Stella enforced her strict rule of school work first. Sometimes the other children helped the girls so they could get at the playing more quickly.

Alice making her own fun terrorizing a chicken in Eaton, 1910. Old Dickerson photo.

Having few toys, the little girls had to create their own fun—
when they had time to play. Lacking the real thing, it was handy
to dress their dog up like a doll. But the dog kept running off and
tearing up the clothes he was supposed to be proudly wearing.
They used a dishpan for a sled and loved sliding down hills in it.
In fact, Helen liked it so much she slid down the gravel in the
summertime, which drove Alice wild because she hated the sound
of metal on gravel. She would say, "Helen, cut that out; you're
getting on my nerves." But Helen slid on.

*Stella, Helen
and Alice.
Photo by Earl
Dickerson,
1913.*

Periodically they tried to break a calf either to ride or pull a
sled in an apparent effort to find the ultimate cooperative calf. No
luck. The calves always ran off.

The girls were not above getting into mischief. One of Alice's
most vivid memories of childhood boo-boos was when her father
one day commanded her to get off a wagon, where she had been
told she could not play. She promptly jumped off and mashed a
baby goose, for which she was soundly spanked. Funny how one
remembers those times even after eight decades. Alice also aggravated her grandpa because she was forever asking questions, a
curiosity trait she never lost as long as she lived. Grandpa usually
ended one of those sessions by assailing her with a gruff "Oh, shut
up." Alice also had a habit of running off, for which her mother
tied her to a doorknob for awhile.

Cora, Stella, Alice and Helen enjoyed walking to the Buckhorn to fish and pick berries up in the rock ravines. The girls carried in their pockets fish lines wound on a little stick. They caught grasshoppers and, when they were ready to fish, cut willow poles. Always, following a fire, berries flourished. After the Sherwood fire the hills were alive with raspberries and huckleberries. One day the Earl Dickersons' and their cousins took tubs and went picking. While the adults were picking, Alice, age 8, Helen, age 7, and cousins Howard and Ethyl decided they would have some lunch. They opened the picnic baskets and ate all they wanted, giving the

Alice eating pancakes while tied to a doorknob.
Photo by Stella Dickerson, 1911.

rest to the dogs. All that was left was a can or two of sardines. Soon the adults came back dead tired and hungry as bears. "They'd liked to have killed us," Alice said, still feeling badly about their devilment. "We should have known better."

Stella did not worry much about her little daughters if they had run off to Uncle Mack's in his old log cabin a mile down the road. Especially on Sundays they ran down there, because every Sunday he baked light bread and rolls for his weekly supply and always gave the girls fresh hot homemade bread with butter. Uncle Mack baked bread on the wrong day once and never heard the end of it. Probably he made his own yeast, as many home-steaders did, because Fleischmann's did not exist then.

Another favorite pastime of the girls was going to their grandmother's house across the field to stay all night. "Her featherbed was heavenly," said Alice. "We could bury ourselves in it. Sometimes she'd take hot irons and wrap them in a quilt or something to warm our feet in bed. I loved sleeping with her in that bed."

"It was always cold in that house," Alice recalled. "The knives and forks were so cold they stuck to my mouth. Grandma had to warm them so they could be eaten off of, they were so frosty." Once Grandma asked Alice how many pancakes she could eat. "Six,"Alice answered confidently. But when the pancakes were set in front of her, she could get only 1½ down. When her chagrined grandmother questioned her, Alice said, making a circle with thumbs and fingers, "Mom's are only this big."

The girls were required to help as much as they could, bringing in wood, feeding chickens and other chores. They never minded it and made play out of the work any time an opportunity arose. They wanted to help, even when tiny little bits of girls. One day when Helen was barely able to talk, the

Grandpa's house.

family was traveling in the spring wagon over Sherwood Hill. Suddenly the team balked and started backing downhill. A crate of chickens they were hauling broke and chickens went flying all over. "Pop was swearing," laughed Alice, "and we were all running around trying to catch chickens. Pop was furious. Helen tried to help him swear and said, 'I'm gun tinkle on that pitty yok over theah.' She was going to fix that rock and help her daddy." A favorite marble dresser top broke in that accident—the horses finally turned the wagon over. Who knows where all the chickens went, but at least little Helen made everybody laugh.

The old Lytle soddy was used for a blacksmith shop for several years. The girls did not go barefooted often, but one day Alice slipped into the shop with not even a sock on to watch her dad work with the hot irons. She stepped on some black hot iron scraps. They stuck to her feet and she couldn't shake them off as she became quite audible. "That did hurt," she said; "If they had been red hot, they would have slipped off."

In June, 1914, while Earl, Stella and children were visiting in Eaton, they attended a circus in Greeley in which Buffalo Bill was a participant. Alice said, "Someone threw balls up, probably glass. Buffalo Bill was riding his white horse carrying a rifle and he shot at the balls. He hit all but one. The only reason he missed the one was because he saw a little boy up in a tree in line with his would-be shot, so he deliberately missed. I loved that show."

Earl would not allow the girls to handle a play gun any differently than they would the real thing. He took Alice rabbit hunting when she was small and taught her how to safely use a .22 rifle. Later, when she had reached the age of 10, he bought her a .410 shotgun, knowing she was competent in gun skills and safety.

Buffalo Bill shooting balls in the air. From booklet,"A Peep at Buffalo Bill's Wild West,"1887.

Cover of booklet, "A Peep at Buffalo Bill's Wild West", 1887. McLoughlin Bros., New York.

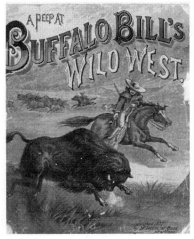

Snow

Five feet of snow kept Earl on the go
Fetching family and horses their feed;
A neighbor brought flour at just the right hour
And Earl shot a deer for their need.
December to March it froze stiff as starch
But they toughed it out in the cold;
With turnips and foul meat they at least did eat
And the horses were strong, lean and bold.

Winter, 1913, was the first the Dickersons stayed up on the homestead. Earl was busy that fall helping to run a telephone line to Hourglass Lake, so he put off going to town for supplies. Tom Bennett had persuaded Earl to wait and they would both go to town.

Earl, Tom and Frank Koenig built that first line for the Hourglass Lake Company from Hourglass Lake, through the Gold Nugget, which was later called Beaver Flat, and still later Sky Ranch, down past the Derby place, now called the Lazy D Ranch, past the Little South Poudre River, up the old Pennock Pass road, which originally went straight up and down over the pass, and across the south corner of Dickersons' hayfield. It connected there with the Forest Service line and continued on along the road to the Buckhorn Ranger Station and the Estes Park Trail. The Lake Company had a caretaker up at the lake and needed a phone so he could communicate with Greeley about irrigation water releases. The Hourglass Lake line joined the Rockwell line above the Dickerson house. Thus people on both spurs, Rockwell and Hourglass, had a means to communicate with the outside world.

Sam, Cora and Allen were in Eaton. It had been a beautiful fall and Earl, Stella and their two children were enjoying the novelty of starting to live in the mountains year round. Then it hit. They awoke on December 1 to beautiful snowflakes descending straight down past the windows of their tiny cabin. It continued on through the day and the next day and finally stopped after piling five feet deep. Earl, Tom and Frank had just about finished their work when the storm hit. Mother Nature must have been testing the grit of these novice homesteading mountaineers.

The grim reality of what was in store soon penetrated Earl's mind; he should have taken the time to go to town for supplies, as

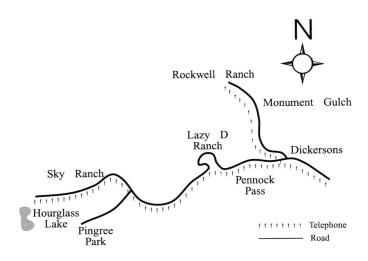

Hourglass Lake vicinity.

turnips were about all he and his family had to eat. His horses needed to be fed. They all could starve if he couldn't get to town. They had very little flour and little fuel for their lamps, which he had casually mentioned to Ranger Walt Brown. He decided he would have to get to town. But he could not. Nobody could. And he would have been in a mess even if he could have made it to Fort Collins.

According to the December 5, 1913 **Fort Collins Morning Express**, snowfall on December 1 exceeded all previous records with 31 inches. *"Only three Decembers in 42 years have shown more precipitation than has fallen in the last four days,"* the publication reported. *"Plows with eight and sixteen horses were tried in clearing off crossings and proved a failure."* Then they hired sixty men and supplied them with shovels. *"City prisoners refused to work and will get the bread and water diet for some days to come. All of the unemployed of the city found employment yesterday without difficulty, as men were in demand as shovelers and at good wages. From 30 to 50 cents an hour was offered for men to shovel, those working on the housetops drawing the higher wages for the additional danger they incurred."*

And in the **Fort Collins Courier**, *"Not in the history of the state as far as records or memory of men go has there ever been such a storm as engulfs the city and the entire state as well.*

34

During this week there has been a snowfall of 31", with an inch of water to each foot of snow. At one time yesterday, it was necessary to put sixteen horses on a large snow plow, but it was found that little could be accomplished, as the snow only piled up in front of it, so the smaller plow was brought into use, with four teams to pull it."

Old log horse barn. Old Dickerson stereoscope photo, date unknown.

Meanwhile, back at the ranch up the Buckhorn, the Dickersons ran out of kerosene and had no light at all for a few days. Then appeared a man on skis walking on top of it all; it was Ranger Brown from the Ranger Station. He brought a gallon of kerosene to Earl and told him there was an eight-point buck just down the hill; it was exhausted, and he told Earl to go get it. Never having shot a deer, Earl protested a bit, but Walt convinced him he would need the meat. Dusk was near, so Earl donned some skis he had made from boards and, with gun in hand, approached the buck, still submerged in the deep snow even after Walt had passed him twice. He shot it, then returned to the barn to feed the horses before returning to dress the deer. Stella was in the barn doing her best to take care of things, but it was getting dark.

It was so dark by the time they finished chores that Earl could not see the ridge of snow bordering the deep trail he had shoveled so he could get the horses to water. He stumbled and plunged head first into the trail, his skis having caught in the ridge. There he was, skis crossed on top of the snow ridge and standing on his head in the bottom of the deep trail. Every move he made to uncross the skis knocked more snow down onto his face and neck. Stella doubled over laughing but soon thought better of that when she realized Earl was not laughing. "Damn it, I can't laugh," snarled Earl. "It isn't funny." Between the two of them they straightened out the skis and, very tired, went back to the house. In a blue funk Earl decided to leave dressing the buck until the next morning. When he got to it, the buck was still standing, so packed in the snow he could not drop. Earl dressed it and got it back to the house. The meat tasted so bad and tough that the family could hardly eat it. But they eventually ate it all, like it or not, as it was better than nothing and at least filling.

Earl's snowbound buck's antlers. Photo by Elyse Bliss, 1993.

About the only other food item in stock was turnips, and Mr. Bennett had 500# of flour at the ranger station which he had told the Dickersons to borrow until they were able to return it. At least they were well-nourished and did not starve. Earl went to get the flour and brought back as much as he could on his back. Alice described the ordeal rather emphatically: "That deer meat was about the nastiest stuff I ever ate. We had that and turnips and I didn't like them then and I still don't like them very well. I was only five years old and I still remember eating that stuff."

After the snow settled a lot, John Derby, who lived a few miles below Dickersons, took his herd of cattle down to the valley. They led some horses through first to make a trail for the cattle to follow. After the cattle were gone, Earl went down to get hay, which he had raised and stacked the previous summer on the State land west of the Hammond field. He tied tight a huge bundle of hay, somehow got it up onto his shoulders and got it to the road. But when he tried to walk in the now-frozen cattle tracks, he wrenched his knee backwards, injuring it. Somehow, though, he staggered home with the hay. Not wanting to go through that again, he made some sled runners, fastened some bedsprings on them and made a lightweight sled. He hitched his ingenious sled to his horses and successfully moved hay from the lower hayfield up to his barn.

Meanwhile, in Eaton, Grandpa and Allen were chomping at the bit to get back up to the homestead. Leaving Cora, they left Eaton in the spring wagon. When they arrived at the Haymaker cabin, it was too drifted to continue with the wagon, so they left it there and rode the horses up to the homestead, harness and all, and they were glad to get home.

A couple of days after the men had arrived, Earl tied a roll of bedding, a suitcase, some food for his family and hay for the horses onto his homemade sled. Then he, Stella, Helen and Alice set out for Eaton. It was a wild trip, with horses plunging through the steep, sloping crusted snowdrifts. When the animals lost their footing and went down, Earl used a pole to help get them on their feet again. Anything not tied onto the sled rolled off, including the little girls and their mama. They spent the night at the Haymaker cabin, then left the sled there and went the rest of the way in the spring wagon. It was a grueling, long trip. The sled remained where they had left it for years afterwards.

Not long after that Grandpa and Allen arrived in Eaton with the other team of horses. It was March, and their first winter on the homestead had been an enlightening one.

After a few days getting settled in Eaton and feeling festive, Earl took the family to the (silent) picture show one evening. As they left the theatre, Earl collided with a seat, further damaging his wounded knee. He did not walk again until they returned to the homestead that summer. It was to plague him the rest of his life, but he worked hard in spite of it. He could not bend it enough even to tie his shoe and eventually developed arthritis, so he always walked with a cane.

Sam, Cora and Allen had gone up earlier in the spring and planted the oats, potatoes and garden. Earl and his family returned in early summer.

Probably the Mummy winked at Mother Nature as if to say, "I think they've got what it takes........don't you?"

School Days

Stella went down to Masonville town
To place her two daughters in school;
She rented one day a place they could stay
And the girls thought the school was cool.
Then the road washed out which cast some doubt
'Bout the soundness of the Buckhorn trail;
So home they stayed and Mama gave aid
From the Calvert home school in the mail.

The time came for Alice and Helen to go to school. They lived twenty four miles up from Masonville, the nearest place for them to attend, which meant they would have to move down during the winter months. So, about the beginning of World War I, Stella Dickerson and her two daughters moved over the rocks and through the creeks down the Buckhorn to Masonville so the girls could begin their education.

They lived here and there before buying a lot next to the Masonville Church upon which they eventually built a house. Both girls were in the same class, though Helen was 16 months younger. They sometimes walked about a mile to school.

While the children were in school, Stella worked at odd jobs to make a little money. Earl, too, found jobs here and there in Masonville after the snow made it impossible to continue working on the homestead.

Masonville, a small community, was nevertheless a busy place in those days when live horsepower was still the main means of transportation. The store was a half a mile west of where it was to be in later years and near a large barn where homesteaders stalled their horses overnight while taking their loads of posts, poles and logs upon which bridge planks were to be laid, called "stringers", to town. Stella ran the boarding house one year, feeding the hungry men tired from the day's drive down the Buckhorn. One time Stella was sick and Earl cheerfully pinch hit for her and fed the boarders pickled pigsfeet, which were gone in a flash. Stella had worked very hard fixing them for her family and was not just mildly upset. He never did that again.

Earl and Allen were batching up at the ranch off and on while Stella and the girls were in Masonville. One night Earl heard what

Masonville Store and Post Office, 1915. Old Dickerson stereoscope photo. Hotel on far side, barely visible, is where the Kitchens lived; partial building on near side is where Stella boarded people.

he guessed was a packrat in the pantry. He picked up a piece of stove wood and quietly opened the door, then quickly closed it. "A civit cat," he announced to Allen. Civit cat is a nickname for the Spotted Skunk or, for the scientific-minded, ***Spilogale putorius***. Earl's next strategy was to put a piece of meat in a tall bucket so the critter could not get out and they would carry it outside. After that failed, they set a lamp in the attic and decided that when they heard it in there, deadeye Allen would shoot it. That worked. He shot both the skunk and the lamp. Whew! Their next strategy was to contain the odor. They closed the attic door, keeping the odor up there, threw the corpse out in the meadow and the crisis was over. Next morning Ranger Willey came to call on his way to town and let his dog out for a run. The dog immensely enjoyed rolling on the skunk, so the ranger had a splendid trip to town.

Alice and Helen, in their second year of school, sat on a hay wagon by the Masonville Store in the evenings after school

Masonville Store, Will Kitchen standing in front. 1916. Photo by Mrs. Hedberg.

watching a fire burning on Sherwood Hill. Mr. Sherwood had let a fire get away from him and the blaze, out of control, created a brilliant evening sky. The girls, awestricken, wondered if their father, uncle and grandpa fighting the fire would be burned up. Fortunately, they were not.

They also watched, sometime between 1920 and 1923, the store moved to its present position. The girls had always enjoyed watching Will and Elick Kitchen bringing their wagonloads of posts and poles to their pole yard by the store before it was moved.

Mr. Heinz, who with his two grown daughters lived on Crystal Mountain, stopped one day in Masonville and gave Alice and Helen some Belgian Hare rabbits, two does and a buck. That began a rabbit raising project up at the homestead later on after the girls were out of school.

The Masonville School was a long, one room, 20x40' white, trimmed-with-green frame building with a row of windows on each side. Along one side near the center stood a large coal heating stove with a jacket around it. Across the business end of the room stretched a blackboard.

The girls remembered fondly some of their classroom days. Typically a teacher required 10-minute recitation periods from each student. At the front of the room was a recitation bench, upon which the student sat when called upon by the teacher. At other times if a student was called upon and did not know the answer, he or she stayed in at recess. Occasionally the teacher acquired a

Recess, Masonville School. 1916.   *Photo by Mrs. Hedberg.*

student like Alice, who enjoyed sitting in school and reading the Big Webster Dictionary—that and crossword puzzles and lexi-con—so much that the teacher had to order her to go out and play during both mid-morning and mid-afternoon recess. The children brought lunches, but occasionally had stew or soup prepared on the big heating stove.

Modern Health Crusader's

CERTIFICATE OF ENROLLMENT

★

*T*HIS Certifies That   *Alice Dickerson*

Has done at least 75% of the Crusaders' health chores for the number of weeks required for first honors in health knighthood; has agreed to try (1) to do nothing that may hurt the health of any other person, (2) to help keep home and town clean, and (3) to keep the Crusaders' health rules until the end of December following this school year; and, therefore, is enrolled until then as a Modern Health Crusader with the title of Squire.

_____ *Dec 23* _____ 192*1*   *Mrs J. W. Roswell*
                                                  Crusader Master (Teacher)

Health Rules

1. Keep windows open or stay outdoors when you sleep, play, work or study. Breathe *fresh* air always and through your nose. Take deep breaths every day, with exercise.

2. Play and exercise daily. If you are undernourished, have a rest period in the daytime and exercise only lightly.

3. Eat wholesome food, including fruit, coarse breads, whole-grain cereals, and vegetables such as carrots, onions and greens. Avoid fried foods, soggy breads, pickles, spices; much meat, pie crust, cake and sweets; and all impure candy. Chew thoroughly. Have three meals a day. Drink, slowly, at least two glasses of unskimmed milk, pasteurized or pure. Drink plenty of pure water.

4. Wash your hands always before eating or handling food. Wash ears, neck and face and clean your fingernails every day. Bathe your whole body twice a week at least and shampoo often. Brush your teeth thoroughly after breakfast and supper. Remove food between teeth. Have all cavities in your teeth filled. Consult a dentist twice a year. Have a complete physical examination each year. Have a regular time every day for attending to toilet. Through right diet and exercise see that you eliminate freely.

5. Get a long night's sleep, going to bed at an early, regular time.

6. Keep fingers, pencils and everything likely to be unclean out of your mouth and nose. Drink no tea, coffee nor drinks containing injurious drugs. Do not smoke or use tobacco in any form.

7. Keep your mind clean. Be cheerful and courageous. Be sincere in what you say.

8. Sit and stand up straight. Lying down, be long. Hold reading matter not less than 12 nor more than 18 inches from your eyes; if less or greater distance is "natural," consult an oculist.

9. Be helpful to others. Whenever you cough or sneeze, turn your head aside and cover your mouth with your handkerchief. If you must spit, spit only where it will be removed before person or fly can touch it. Keep your clothes and books neat. Brush your shoes before school.

Helen and Alice especially liked their journeys to the Buckhorn Presbyterian Church at Masonville, which had been built in 1909.

"When we were in the first grade the Masonville minister, Reverend Moore, would come up to where we were living. He'd come with a sled on very cold mornings and he had sleighbells on his horse. He'd take us to Sunday School on that sled and we thought that was wonderful. He'd put a lap robe over us. He was the first minister in Masonville," recalled Helen.

Buckhorn Presbyterian Church as it was then.

One person who stayed permanently etched into their memories was Mrs. Ed Smith (Sarah). Not only did they love her as a Sunday School teacher, but she came to the one room, eight class school in her late years and talked to the children about pioneering. Mrs. Smith had come with her husband to Colorado by ox team. One thing Helen remembered was how she said they had made their floor of clay, wetting it and packing it down until it was smooth and slick. Then, when it was dry, it was so hard it could be scrubbed.

The Smiths had a homestead on Crystal Mountain and pastured big herds of Black Angus cattle in the summer. They had previously owned a dairy herd, but had sold that and invested in two full-blooded Angus breeding bulls, which became the foundation of the high-grade Angus cattle they ran on their ranches. In the winter they moved them down to their ranch in Masonville. Sarah's son-in-law was the first teacher in the tiny community.

Sarah never forgot the Dickerson girls at Christmas during the winters they couldn't get down for school. There was always a box with interesting things in it for their Christmas. The girls remembered a Christmas party at the church when tragedy was averted by alert, quick thinking. "At that time they didn't have colored lights. They used small candles in holders, and when they were lighting the candles, the tree caught on fire. The grownups got the fire out before it did a lot of damage, but there was a lot of scrambling before it was completely doused."

A big threshing machine topped by a big iron hood often came puffing along through Masonville while the little girls were living there. It frightened Helen so that she would run and hide. Little did the girls know that years later their family would buy the big steam engine from Roy Hyatt, without the hood, to power their sawmill.

The month of May brought a homeward trip to the homestead for the summer. But in the summer of 1923, a giant flood gutted the Buckhorn Canyon and left no road, just a creek bed. There was not a road to the Poudre from Pennock Pass, either, although work had begun with teams of horses. Stella, Helen and Alice could not go anywhere for two years; school was out. Grandmother Cora was bedridden by that time, having been afflicted by a stroke, which was another reason Stella stayed home.

When just horses were used to rebuild a road, progress was not very swift. The men went horseback over Hahn Hill, about six miles east of Dickersons, to Stove Prairie when necessary and brought supplies back in panyards on horses. Stella, determined to educate her daughters as much as possible, enrolled them in the Calvert School course from Maryland. The horses carried reports to be sent to and from the school through the Masonville Post Office. Stella benefited almost as much as the girls, because she, too, had not had a whale of a lot of formal education. When the girls did go back to school they were promoted from the 3rd to the 5th grade and were told that some of the things they learned from the Calvert School were high school courses.

After finally giving up going to the Masonville one-room school, they spent the rest of their lives educating themselves both through extensive reading and practical everyday living skills and knowledge. Both Alice and Helen have always been quick to say that their seven hectic years of on-again, off-again formal school education was supplemented by lessons learned in the school of "hard knocks and awkwardness".

Raging Waters

Colorado is dry, but in the blink of an eye
It can rain 'til the creeks run full;
To a high degree in the year twenty three
The Buckhorn roared like a bull.
The flood washed out bridges and flattened some ridges
So the road was just rocks and debris;
Too tough for a wagon—teams would be draggin';
It was years 'til a new road would be.

Early in 1923 a week of hard, steady rain combined with heavy snows melting from the previous winter caused a massive flood in the Buckhorn. It washed out bridges and reduced what had been a beautiful trail up the creek to a rocky channel filled with rocks and debris, twenty feet deep in places. It also took out the little trail to Estes Park and its beautiful little bridges. All seven of the Dickersons had been at the homestead when the flood raged down the canyon; it is an advantage to be up at the top when such a catastrophe takes place.

It took six years to rebuild bridges and repair the road, so everyone had to take horses and travel over the mountaintops, including Sherwood Hill, just as they did in the earlier days before there was a road at all. The Dickerson men would be gone a week and haul what supplies and food they could in horse-borne panyards. In the winter, Earl, Allen, Roscoe Moore and Mr. Sherwood took pack horses over the Hahn Mountains to Masonville to get groceries and mail. Snows were too deep to consider going by way of the Poudre.

Roscoe Moore, a Buckhorn homesteader, tried taking his team and wagon up on the mountain. The horses spooked, bolted and ran away with the wagon, dumping Moore on the ground. He finally found his horses, but took some time finding his wagon, which was quite battered. He would have been better off to take saddle horses with panyards to town rather than to risk travel by wagon on the primitive, abandoned high mountain trail.

After the canyon road washed out, Dickersons were going home over Sherwood Hill one winter day. The hill was slick with snow and they met a truck coming down the steepest part. There was no room to pass, and the truck could not stop. The girls' cousin, Lyle Smith, backed his load of mine props down the hill

45

as fast as he could while the other truck careened down like a sled, not a wheel moving. One front wheel slipped over the bank and everybody jumped out to hurriedly push it back up onto the road. Sam Dickerson slipped and fell under the truck just as it slid back up. His foot was under the moving front wheel, but luckily it was sideways and his shoes had heavy soles, so he wasn't hurt too badly. Lyle succeeded in getting his truck backed to the foot of the hill just in the nick of time as the other truck slid silently by, its driver glued to the steering wheel, not looking left or right.

When the repairs and rebuilding were finished in 1929, another narrow Buckhorn Canyon road served the travelers.

The Estes Park Trail was rebuilt by the Forest Service, but up on the hillsides rather than in the valleys. After the flood devastation, the original trail was difficult to even locate. The new trail was re-named the Danner Hill Trail.

Inside The Cabin

Coal oil made lights to brighten the nights
And a wood stove heated their toes.
The girls slept outside; under quilts they'd hide
They arose with bare feet in the snow.
The wood stove was warm, relief from a storm
But the outhouse had no heat at all;
Doors were not locked, so in strangers walked
If they needed a shelter of wall.

Life at the homestead was never easy. The altitude at the Dickerson home was precisely 8402'. Winter came earlier and lasted longer than from whence they had come. There was no electricity, refrigeration, gas pipeline, plumbing nor any other convenience to which modern Americans have become accustomed. It was a hard life and required perseverance, determination, love of family, a faith in God and a willingness to work hard.

Stella found she could breathe better than anyplace else she had been in her life, so she became content with the hardships and did the best she could to keep her family supplied with good food, clothing, warmth, education and love.

Until other additions were built, the kitchen was the original cabin. They made a Murphy bed on the east wall that hung up in the daytime and down at night. Doors and windows were changed and rooms added on at different times through the years.

Originally little Helen and Alice slept on the south porch, later enclosed inside the walls of the cabin, but at that time a screened-in porch. Their bed was a sort of lounge that could be raised on either side or both, whichever was desired and in their earliest homestead days they slept out there year round, even when it snowed. Their parents unrolled a canvas curtain above them when they went to bed, which the girls would promptly get up and roll back up again so they could look at the stars which were as brilliant as could be. Alice said, "Snow blew in on the floor and bed and there would be frost on our faces and hair. We'd

47

come running into the house with our bare feet in the snow. We didn't catch cold all winter."

Lighting the homes in the early days was a problem. Some used candles, but most used coal oil with the #2 burner. The Rayo lamp made a pretty good light, according to Helen and Alice, but it used so much coal oil that most people used it just for special occasions. Also, it was a problem transporting coal oil up to the homestead without spilling it on the groceries. Helen said, "They usually pushed a raw potato down on the can spout and set it in a pasteboard box wrapped in a gunny sack, but with juggling on the rough road in a wagon, some of the food was generally flavored, especially flour and sugar."

As was common anywhere in those days with no indoor plumbing, the facility was a little vertical building with tiny side screened windows for ventilation containing a wooden seat with one, two or three holes in it. They did have "chamber mugs" for temporary use inside when it was inconvenient or too cold to use the outhouse ... or "backhouse" as the Dickerson family called it.

A Majestic wood stove with two trivets and a warming oven was the heat source for the tiny cabin. The trivets served as handy places to keep bacon and pancakes warm while the rest of the food was being prepared. If the night was cold, someone would get up and replenish the fire; otherwise, it could get very cold by morning.

They also had two or three Quickmeal stoves, which were obviously their favorite brand, through the years. Stella had one with a reservoir and when water had to be packed a long way they stuffed it with icicles instead. After waiting until they dripped off the roof awhile, removing any dirt, they could select beautiful, clear icicles.

The busy Dickersons were not too particular at first about what kind of wood they burned; Earl did not care—just get it here, there was too much else to do to worry about that. Wood was cut by hand as they did not have a buzz saw.

An ice house was built so ice could be kept all summer and sometimes all fall, but at first they did not even have an icebox. The ice house floor was sawdust and the center, surrounded by and covered over with sawdust, held the ice. Cutting it was an awful job. Alice would go with her dad in the wagon down the Buckhorn to get the cold, heavy, slippery stuff when she was big enough to help. Just a little square 4' deep weighed over 200#. Before a block was removed for use in an icebox, the sawdust all had to be wiped off.

Quickmeal stove in Dickerson kitchen.

No one locked doors in those days; it was an unspoken law of the land that cabins provided refuge and nourishment for wayfarer emergencies. Even when they left the homestead so the girls could go to school the houses were left open. People had respect for homes belonging to other people, and owners trusted that anyone entering their home needed to, or they would not have. Food was left in the unlocked Dickerson cabin not only in case someone was stranded and needed help, but so Earl could "batch" when he went up for a load of timber. Their house was used many times and the food would be gone, so none of the Dickersons ever came home without food; they always had some on hand. They were more than repaid the following summer when people who had stayed there, mostly farmers from the valley coming to get posts or large timbers, brought fruit and vegetables they knew could not be raised by the Dickersons at their high altitude. Those, indeed, were the good—old—days. All over Western America, including Canada, that was the rule, as expressed in "The Unwritten Law of the Yukon":

> *Nothing shall be locked.*
> *A hungry, cold man is always welcome.*
> *If the owner of a cabin is away, a stranger may come*
> *in and make himself at home.*
> *Never leave a cabin without leaving dry kindling wood,*
> *matches and without cleaning up.*
> *When necessary, a man may help himself to a food cache,*
> *providing he leaves a note saying what*
> *He took and when he will return it.*
> *Do unto others as you would be done by.*

The Dickerson home.   Photo by Helen Dickerson, 1935.

Clothing

They always looked nice, 'cause grime was a vice
  'cept Allen—he delighted in dirt.
But that was his loss...he lacked a boss—
  A woman to keep him alert.
Stella wore long dresses which seldom were messes
  And the girls wore ribbons in their hair.
She boiled clothes on the stove and they cleaned, by Jove;
  Then she pressed them with a flatiron on a chair.

The Dickerson menfolk, except for Allen, were never ragged or dirty. Few others of the mountain folk were either. Sam Dickerson rarely went a day without wearing a tie. As soon as he had shaved in the morning he put one on, no matter what work he had planned. They wore neatly patched, cleaned and pressed clothes at a time in history when work was extremely rough on clothing, not to mention the toil required to wash and iron the garments. But Allen was an exception; when he went into the service in 1918 to participate in World War I, Alice said, "He was real neat when he was in the service, but after he got out he was nice and slovenly again. Wore old dirty cloths and slouchy.

World War I. Picture taken just before going overseas, Oct.21, 1918.
Allen is in lower left corner of "B" in "Bought".

He wanted to look like a ragamuffin; my cousin Ethyl called him 'my friend, Pigpen.'"

The women, too, endeavored to look nice. Stella wore long dresses and made nice clothes for her daughters. She wanted them

Ribbons in their hair. Helen and Alice Dickerson.   Photo by Stella, 1913.

to look neat and she always tied ribbons in their hair. She had a treadle Singer sewing machine and was quite proficient in taking apart clothes that had been given to her and making them over for the girls. Grandma Cora always wore a sunbonnet, apron, her one pair of half-moon earrings and a key-shaped pin; she felt she was not dressed without them.

Sometimes feed sacks were used for overshoes when it was cold and the snow was not melting. They cut down the sack seams, folded them under their shoes for thickness underneath, over the shoetops, then wound them up over the trouser legs as far as desired and secured them with heavy twine, wire or nails. Though these not-so-fancy overshoes did not wear very long, there were always more gunny sacks and they were warmer than overshoes.

Alice and Helen wore Lisle (hard, twisted cotton thread woven to make stockings, gloves and other items) stockings, but they did not last very long, sometimes not even a trip to town. The little girls wore shoes with buckles that reached above the ankles and a button hook had to be used to get them on and off. Alice and Helen hated them because of all the procedure and "they looked horrible."

Stella boiled the white clothes, including sheets, in a boiler on the stove, but the boiling water had to be watched carefully. Alice said, when recalling the years of clothes-washing in their kitchen, "I've always told people not to let boiling water get out and under the teakettle, because it will break the lids. They crack and 'BOOM!!'—it sounds like a gun going off. It was the same with the boilers."

They didn't have soap powder in those days; Stella used Fels Naptha, bars of yellowish or green soap, which she would shave up and scatter into the boiler. When hanging out the articles to dry, sometimes they would get as hard as a board, so she would leave them until the next day...or the next...or next. She ironed the clothes, but not the bed linens, with flatirons. When the irons were placed on the stove she always had a piece of paper or rag with which to wipe them off, so the clean clothes would not get soiled. Their ironing board, upon which sat the trivet for the iron, did not have legs, so she and the girls set it on a table and chair.

Food — Meat

Within the shed a calf was dead
*   Pop hung it so it would cool;*
Alice grabbed her gat, said "we've got a rat!"
*   Whap! And the boiler lid blew.*
Helen said, "tis the bunk, I smell a skunk."
*   Pop said, "give me that gat!"*
He shot the thing and his nose did sting
*   'Twas a civit cat, not a rat!*

Food storage was a problem without refrigeration. If meat was brought up from town in the summertime, it would be put on to cook and thoroughly heated, then cooled overnight. Next day it was reboiled and they used what they needed for that day before storing the remainder in the cellar. Each day thereafter they cooked it until it was very hot; eventually it was used up.

Stella canned meat in big boilers, particularly if a beef was butchered in the summer. Some of it they put in a stone jar of brine and other portions they smoked, dried or made into corned beef. For smoking they used burning willows, letting the smoke go up through a pipe and out into a big wooden box where the meat was hung. Many people salted meat instead of canning it because they did not have pressure cookers.

In winter meat was hung out in the cold. It kept for a long time if hung in the shed; a kind of rind formed on the outside. If it was frozen, it kept all winter. Even if it was not frozen it kept a long time if air was allowed to circulate around it.

"If it thawed, blood started dripping and the freezing and thawing made it tough like whang leather, but still chewable," laughed Alice. "Just cut off a hunk when needed. We didn't have a problem with animals getting to it, because it was always in a shed...in the shade, where it kept cool. People used to say they could hang it up so high in a tree that even the flies couldn't get it, but I don't believe that."

One time Earl butchered a calf and hung it in the shed to cool. "I think we have a rat (packrat) in there," stated Alice.

"I'm not too sure," Helen replied. "I think I smell a skunk."

With that, Alice shot at it, missed and hit the boiler lid instead. Earl said, "Give me that gun," and he shot. Sure enough it was a civit cat and its fumes drove Earl swiftly out the door. Alice thought the meat would be ruined, but it was not, even though all utensils had to be scoured because they tasted like skunk smelled.

The Dickersons bought meat the same as everybody else did, but the cheapest parts they could get. Sometimes they had just sowbelly (salt side) and beans. After boiling the sowbelly in water to eliminate the salt, they rolled it in corn meal and fried it like bacon.

Skinning a deer. Alice and Allen, 1930.   *Photo by Helen Dickerson.*

They raised pigs and once in awhile Allen shot a deer. Stella canned pork or salted it and made hams. Some portions they hung in the shed during winter and it became so stiff and cold they had to use an axe or saw to obtain a slice. She also made sausage, some of which was fried and packed in a two-gallon stone jar. She collected the lard and poured it over the sausage, thereby preventing it from spoiling. It was stored in a cold place and not kept too far into the summer. It was, according to Alice, delicious. Some of the side pieces and hams were put into salt brine and smoked like beef. Helen said, "It was tasty, but a little tougher than what people are used to now. Allen used to say it would be a lot tougher if we didn't have it."

They made a lot of mincemeat in the fall during apple season and when a beef was butchered; it made good pies. Stella also canned fish and stored it in the dirt-roofed cellar.

From the three Belgian Hare rabbits the girls had received from Mr. Heinz, they raised rabbits by the hundreds all year long.

"We raised them to sell. Seemed like all we ate was rabbit and I got so I didn't like to even smell them," Alice said. "We sold them to the college at Pingree Park, but they wanted us to dress them for them, which we did. They came over Pennock Pass in their Ford and got them, along with cottage cheese, milk, cream and butter. We had rabbit cages east and south of the house—all over the place. We'd get big bunches of hay for them and in the summer I'd go out and get gunny sacks full of dandelions for them—and grass. We never bought rabbit food. We couldn't, because we didn't have a car. We just gave them what we had; oats, oat hay or whatever. Finally Pop turned the bucks loose thinking when he wanted a rabbit he'd just go out and shoot one, but he didn't because the predators got them——every single one."

Food — Farmyard Vittles

Cows gave milk and cream smooth as silk
  So Stella made butter and cheese.
Folks came to buy it and near caused a riot
  If they couldn't get what they pleased.
She also had chickens and gave them the dickens
  If they didn't lay eggs each day.
She packed eggs in bran in a great big can
  They'd keep a long time that way.

The first few years on the homestead they did not have cows. Either they went without milk or they bought canned milk by the case. However, about the time Alice and Helen returned home after their formal schooling had ended, the family had acquired one cow and a few chickens.

Later on, when their bovine herd had grown, Stella made and sold cheese, butter, cream and buttermilk to neighbors who came to get it. Some of those mountain folk had beef cattle, but not dairy stock, so Dickersons' fresh dairy products were in much demand. Stella formed her dairy cheese into big five-pound blocks and it was reputedly delicious. She had collected USDA bulletins from which she learned how to make the cheese. Her cottage cheese also was delicious sometimes but others not, according to Alice, who explained, "If the weather wasn't good, it didn't turn out right. I don't know why the weather had anything to do with it, but it did." Colorado A & M professors on their way to and from the Pingree Park Forestry School also stopped frequently for cheese and cottage cheese. Charley Mason's store in Loveland wanted all they could get of Stella's rolls of dairy cheese. Charley had been a cattleman on his Buckhorn homestead, but he became afflicted with creeping paralysis and was forced to move to town. Loveland people went up to buy Stella's butter, which she had made in her 7-gallon churn. Mason gave the Dickersons a premium price, fifty cents, for all the butter they could get to him, but it was a problem getting it there until Alice bought her first car.

Preserving eggs was another technique mountain families had to employ in the pre-refrigeration days. Dickersons bought boxes of egg-laying chickens as they needed a good supply of eggs for making cornbread and pancakes. Stella preferred the waterglass method rather than salt to preserve eggs. Waterglass, a substance consisting of sodium or potassium dissolved in water as a viscous sirupy liquid, was placed in a five-gallon jar in which a case (30 dozen) of eggs was submerged. Those eggs, used for baking only, would keep for a year. Another method she used was to coat the eggs with waterglass, then cover them with lard before burying them in bran; they would keep for quite awhile. Oil in the lard sealed the eggs so bacteria could not enter. If she had no bran available, Stella used sawdust, but she preferred bran because sawdust made the eggs taste woody. Cora, Stella and the

Egg carton. Photo by Elyse Bliss.

girls "fixed" the eggs, which meant coating them with oil or bacon grease, whatever was available, then alternating layers of eggs and bran, with a final layer of bran on the top. The problem with preserving them using the salt method was that the eggs broke if the salt became moist.

"You couldn't get the egg out without putting water on the salt, so a lot of eggs were wasted," said Alice.

When the girls were small, Stella wouldn't let them eat any of her big fat bread loaves when they were fresh out of the oven, because they ate too much. The family seldom bought bakery bread; it was too expensive, and too cumbersome to haul the great distance from town by wagon. Stella made an occasional pie, but not too often, because they did not have the money to buy ingredients to make such fancy things.

The girls learned young to bake bread...about 1915. Baking bread in their wood stove was just part of the daily routine, particularly when they had boarders. Having made a potato starter for the yeast, they always kept out a little of it for the next batch of bread. Most everybody in the mountains kept a starter made from either potatoes or flour. A yeast foam, which they bought, was made from corn meal and yeast. When they made bread, a cake of the foam was placed in water with some potato. They let it foam up, set overnight and then made bread in the morning. Quite often they bought 100# of wheat, which they ground a little at a time in their hand-powered coffee grinder, and used it to make bread.

During World War I they bought flour, sugar and a mixture of bran and flour, called shorts, in 100# lots. Muffins and brown bread were made with shorts. In order to buy flour, they had to buy commodities like dried cereals such as barley flour and whole wheat, corn meal and rice, whether

Chicken house behind the garage.

they wanted them or not. Stella tried to make the bread taste good with barley flour, but it was flat. They weren't supposed to have sugar, either; flour and sugar went to the military services. One of the neighbor women bragged around that she was getting plenty of sugar, but after people found out where she was getting it, she obtained it no more. Dickersons used saccharin, which Alice thought was horrible. About ¼ teaspoon on her dish of oatmeal and she almost threw up. She said, "I don't know what that stuff is, but it'd be about the same as eating a scoop shovel full of sugar with a dish of oatmeal. Ugh."

Sam had to have coffee all the time, he thought, but mostly the family drank postum. It was not instant, but the kind boiled in a

Old Postum ad.

percolater. It came in flakes, like coffee. Alice said, "We bought it in boxes and maybe cans, but mostly boxes, and boiled it like coffee. It was like bran and had a plant called chicory in it." Alice also recalled a coffee hint: "If you burn your bread, instead of throwing the crust out, grind it up and make coffee out of it. Burnt crust makes black coffee. Put sugar and cream on it; it tastes pretty fair."

Moffetts, who lived year-round east of the ranger station, decided to try some coffee being advertised at a very low price if purchased at a minimum of 100# lots. Mae rode horseback to all her neighbors and almost everyone thought it a fine idea. The coffee came as unroasted beans, so Dickersons put theirs in big pans in the oven to brown, then ground them in the coffee grinder. They had to be roasted just right.

"If too done, they don't taste good. If not roasted enough they don't bring out the flavor," advised Alice.

Food — Preparation

Like squirrels they preserved so food could be served
All through the winter at meals;
They made jellies and jam and prepared their ham
And canned in jars with good seals.
They baked light breads and slawed cabbage heads;
Grew all their veggies before frost.
Apples they dried and made cider to hide
And smashed some for apple sauce.

Earl liked to make kraut for winter. He would bring up from town two or three 100# feed sacks of cabbage. Stella prepared the heads for slicing and Earl sliced them into a large stone jar. Alice and Helen took turns stomping it with a big wooden stick cut like a wooden potato masher, only larger. It was stomped and salted alternately a little at a time until the jar was filled and the juice was enough to cover the cabbage. Then a plate with a weight on it was placed on top and it was put away to ferment. They used it from the stone crock through winter, but if any was left by spring, it was put in glass jars and sealed.

Food storage cellar.
Photo by Mildred
Camp, 1973.
Loveland Daily
Reporter-Herald.

Stella also canned peas, carrots and string beans. Of course, they stored potatoes and turnips in the cellar. Helen liked turnips, but Alice said they taste like an old rat smells.

When the time was right, the homesteaders fixed picnic dinners, loaded buckets and tubs on wagons and spent a fun-filled day picking berries, such as the day the darling children and their dogs ate all the lunches. Then they spent long hours cleaning and canning the fruit. That was about all the native fruit the mountaineers had. Bears and grouse enjoyed the berry patches, too.

Other fruits— anything that was available, such as chokecherries, strawberries, grapes and plums were eagerly gathered to make jelly, jam and preserves. Mountain folk went down to the orchards in the fall and got several hundred pounds of windfall apples. After hauling them up in wagons, they had to sort and "work them up" right away or they would quickly spoil. The entire Dickerson family worked all day and night immediately after arriving with them. Earl and the girls sorted and peeled while Stella washed jars and cooked and canned the apples. This may seem commonplace, but the stove had to be continually kept hot, both to cook the apples and to heat the water, which had to be carried in from springs or creeks. Some apples they dried by attaching them by threads to hang on the clothesline.

Earl Dickerson, if not completely occupied with other ranch work, always helped Stella with her kitchen chores, including food preparation and cooking; likewise, Stella helped him if he needed it. Whoever was in need of assistance, other family members pitched in.

Once Stella intended to make vinegar from apple juice, but when she went to get the spiced juice, it was gone. Alice and Helen thought it was delicious and claimed they did not remember if they got a little tipsy.

Critters

Cora threw a fit and shouted, "You git!"
When into the house young Allen brought his horse.
Helen liked to ride, but Alice stepped aside
She'd rather "ride shank's mare" (on foot), of course.
When a lion screamed loud, Helen wasn't cowed...
But she wasn't sure just what the sound could be;
She heard the cowbells clank, her lucky stars she thanked
That she found the cows 'fore dark while she could see.

In the spring, Sam and Cora always went out to fix fence; she would help some, but was more of a companion for Sam. He just wanted her with him. For the most part, Cora was a house person;

she did not go outside much, except to take walks with Sam and, when necessary, step outside to heave dishwater from a pan as far as she could.

Cora and Sam Dickerson.
Photo by Ray Dickerson, date unknown.

Uncle Mack thought he had built his log cabin on his homestead, but the Forest Service came along, surveyed it and told him it was on U.S. Government land. It was a little single-room log cabin with a dog house

63

Cora, Allen and Uncle Mack at Mack's original cabin, 1911.
Photo by Sam Dickerson.

and cellar attached, and he had lived in it for many years. The Forest Service told him he would have to tear it down, but it made him so mad, he burned it down! That incensed the Forest Service, but he didn't care. He started another house across the road and lived in it unfinished until one day he had a mishap which was to end his productive life.

Because Mack had been having dizzy spells, he tied himself to the wagon when he took his team and wagon to town with a load of poles, so the danger of his falling off would be minimal. Hammond's horses, like Dickersons', were not the best in the country; they were always balky and running off. They could not afford good horses, so theirs were the culls. One day, on his way home, Mack had a stroke which resulted in paralysis. The horses cut the corner too close on the wooden bridge by Moore's cabin. He got off to unhitch and the horses trampled him. John Derby found him next morning, a bloody and half-frozen man. No one was at the Moore cabin or the ranger station that winter, so Derby took him to the Dickersons'. He turned Hammond's horses loose and, holding Mack between his knees, drove him up to Sam's house. John did not want to bring him to Earl's house, because he knew how fond of Uncle Mack the little girls were, and thought it would be too much of a shock to them. It was anyway, because observant Alice and Helen saw them go by. Stella ran up to Grandpa's. She and Cora dressed his wounds and they got him into bed. Meanwhile, Pat Keller, Derby's son-in-law, streaked to Masonville on his saddle horse to get Ranger Helmick to go up and take Mack to the doctor in his Model T Ford. Pat almost ran his horse to death. But they got Mack there and all their tender, loving care enabled Uncle Mack to live a few more years. The girls saw him only once more when his family brought him up to his cabin for a day or two, at which time they took him to see the Dickerson family and to pet one of his horses which was corraled there.

Dickersons never had a decent horse, except one they raised from a colt. Allen played with the young colt a lot and aroused his mother's wrath by bringing it into the house to give it a sugar lump. Cora would scream at him, "Get that thing out of here!" He was an unusually smart horse, according to Helen and Allen, the ranch horsepeople. For one thing, he figured out how to pull the stopper out of the barn door, go in, open the grain box and help himself. Sam installed a rat trap, thereafter discouraging the now-lumpy-nosed intelligent animal.

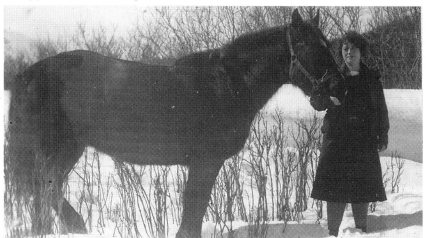

Helen and her favorite horse.   *Photo by Stella, 1930s.*

After he grew up, the colt became Helen's favorite saddle horse. He and Helen always went after the milk cows and, if she did not ride him, she left the reins draped over the saddle horn. She would pick her way through the willows, call him and he would pick his own way and come to her. One time she was leading him at a trot on a narrow trail and she tripped and fell under him; he stopped instantly. Unfortunately, at a later time, he was stricken with sleeping sickness and they found him dead.

In contrast, Helen then rode an Estes Park livery horse, which had been farmed out to the Dickersons following the tourist season. He didn't do anything she wanted him to do and especially would not chase cows. All he wanted to do was follow another horse. One day he ran under a tree limb and bent her backwards over her saddle, hurting her back. Furious, she declared, "This thing won't do what I want him to do," and back to Estes Park he went.

Alice never rode much. She would rather "ride shank's mare", which meant to use her own feet. Nor did she like taking care of livestock. She liked having wild animals around. That may be why she liked her uncle Edwin Foster's Indian broomtail ponies. They were a matched pair of sorrel broncs which he took all over the country and even took them when he went fishing up in the mountains. He had draft horses down in the valley, but the Indian ponies were his joy—they ran like wild animals and it was always exciting when they came.

Helen and Earl milked the cows and she always carried a coal oil lantern when she milked late in the evening or early in the morning. The Dickerson cows were pastured one fall in the Hammond field. They roamed everywhere that time of year searching for bluebonnets and mushrooms, thus making the animals difficult to find and gather. One evening Helen was hunting them up toward White Pine, when a loud scream pierced the calm. Hearing the cowbells clanking in the distance, she kept going, half scared, not knowing the source of the hair-raising scream, and drove the cows home. Later, Ranger Payson asked her if she had heard the mountain lion that evening. Helen gulped, then answered, "I did, but I wasn't sure what it was. I heard the cowbells, so I kept going 'til I found the cows. It was quite late when I got home."

One spring day there was an unfamiliar clatter on the roof. Stumbling over themselves to get outside, Helen and Alice looked up and one of their little calves was looking down at them. Helen ran behind the house, called it and it ran down the other side onto the dirt-covered cellar and executed the short hop to the ground.

A big bull calf was trying to crawl out the barn window one morning and Helen tried to push him back in. He very nearly broke her arm. Alice said, "It's a wonder she wasn't killed. Helen was always getting hurt by one of those animals."

They sold some calves to some people over at the Rockwell Ranch, but when delivery day came, the calves did not want to go. Helen was on her horse, Earl and Alice on foot. Alice, age 19, ran like a modern-day blue heeler dog chasing calves every which way for six miles. She was near exhaustion by the time she completed the round trip back home, twelve miles later, knowing that chores still awaited them. Stella had cooked supper, but first Alice had to chop wood and Helen had to get the cows and do the milking. Alice was in good condition; she could run like a wild animal and was as wiry as they come.

Koenigs' youngest girl required goat's milk, so her parents purchased a pair of goats. After their little herd had grown, Frank took the billy and some of the others up on the Mummy to pasture. When he was bringing them home in the fall, the billy knocked him down so many times he killed the obstinate critter right on the spot where the billy had scored his final knockdown. He left poor old billy there for the wild animals to eat, with not much remorse, saying he would not have tasted good, anyway. After one late deep April snow Koenigs were caught short of feed for milk cows and horses. They had one hundred pounds of pinto beans, so they soaked them to feed the cows. The bovines ate them, but Koenigs said their milk tasted like "nature's remedy". But, at least they did not lose any animals.

Henry Martin lived twelve miles down the Buckhorn from the Dickersons. He ran cattle and trapped for coyotes and bobcats. He caught a bobcat one time by a big rock cliff and, thinking he had killed it, left it in the trap while he re-set the other traps. He was between the cat and the rock ledge when the cat grabbed him and pulled his pants off. Fortunately, trapping was mostly a solitary activity.

Fred Hyatt had a buffalo herd at Cedar Park on Glen Haven road. Some of them escaped and migrated north to Fletcher Hill and bedded down. Some eastern tourists came along and could not get them to move out of the way. But they were thrilled; they thought they had discovered wild buffalo.

Will Gard, a Monument Gulch homesteader and Loveland dairy farmer, one spring drove a big herd of holstein cattle with their first calves up into the mountains, leaving the milk producers down in the valley. Along with the herd, team, wagon and saddle horses were a dozen or more horses and mules to pasture on his homestead. Dickersons always battened the hatches and secured all gates and fences when the advance herders rode ahead to notify them they were approaching; it would have been a real old-time rodeo if their livestock had intermingled with Dickersons' animals.

High Mountain Life

A convict came to call, didn't think they knew at all,
  But Allen showed him how good he was with a gun
They fed the man some food which he certainly didn't elude
  And were glad when he left... he was on the run.
Rockwell had a truck, moved slowly like a duck
  With horses eating hay right off the back;
He drove it in the snow, with horses in front to tow;
  It had solid rubber wheels and that's a fact.

In 1917 there was no road north to the Poudre Canyon from the Rockwell Ranch, only a mountain. One day a fellow appeared from nowhere and walked up to Sam's house. Cora, Allen and Sam were suspicious of the stranger, so Allen, being a crack shot with a rifle, demonstrated his marksmanship before inviting him into their home. After placing a matchstick up on some kind of perch Allen blew the match head off. Allen even shot flies. Hoping the man was sufficiently impressed, they gave him a good supper and put him up for the night. In the morning they fed him breakfast and asked him to mail a letter for them when he got to town. He left in the direction of the Buckhorn Canyon, but the letter never was mailed. They had pegged him for an escaped convict; once in awhile one of them slipped away from over on the Poudre where the prisoners were building the road.

One night a fellow Dickersons knew came to their door. He had spent all day in extremely cold, stormy weather getting a wagon load of poles and had not eaten all day, so he was half-starved and chilled to the bone. After securing his tired team in the barn, he spent the night with Dickersons. Just as he began eating supper, he stiffened out in the chair with sweat rolling down his face. Earl and Stella persuaded him to drink 15 drops of peppermint in water. Soon he revived from his spell and announced he wasn't going to let that fool him out of a good supper.

The Colorado A&M Forestry School, started in Pingree Park in 1916, averaged 80 boys for the school season. Earl Dickerson helped haul their belongings to Pingree Park in his wagon, which was no easy feat; Pennock Pass was straight up and down at that time with no switchbacks.

The first car traveling over the pass was a Stanley Steamer. The first truck hauling a load over the precipitous pass had a pine tree tied to the back so its branches could help the vehicle brake. The driver unhooked the tree across the road from Earl's house. The spot became quite bushy, as each truck thereafter unlashed its tree in the same place.

Grandpa and Allen in Model T. Date and photographer unknown.

Allen, Mr. Sherwood and Ranger Helmick owned the first automobiles up in Dickerson country, all Model T Fords. Allen installed a heavy duty axle on his to make hauling and hill climbing easier. When winter came, water had to be drained from the radiator as there was no antifreeze in those days. If there was a need to use the cars, they had to replenish the water. This annoyance persuaded them to make very few cold weather town trips. Orr Rockwell soon followed suit, purchasing a truck with solid rubber tires. He drove so slowly that Dickersons' horses walked along eating hay off of it. But at least he could get it through Monument Gulch which at that time, 1913-1917, was quite difficult. Sometimes in the winter he would come as far as the Dickersons' with a team of horses hitched in front of the truck to get it through the snow. His wife and daughter would visit for awhile, then ride the horses back home upon the harness, with no saddle.

One day in 1925 Earl was cutting hay in the ranger station field when an airplane flew over, the first ever to fly over their place. He pulled up the horses and stared in awe at the low-flying plane. Back at the cabin, Alice heard it and went running out to see it. She knew instantly it was Charles Lindbergh, because she had heard he was coming; he had joined the Mil-Hi Circus and intended to perform in Colorado and Wyoming county fairs.

Frequently Earl had to deliver lumber over the pass with his team and wagon. Alice often went with him, mainly so she could slip off and go fishing. After leaving Bennetts' ranch there were

no bridges, so it could be rough going up to Hourglass Lake. Tom Bennett, a lake stockholder, hauled fish in 10-gallon milk cans on his wagon. He had fashioned a fish hatchery on what is now Poudre Springs, bought trout eggs and put them in troughs. Water had to be changed frequently while en route, as it was a long trip. Pat Keller hung a milk can on each side of a pack saddle and took the little fingerlings to the Mummy Range lakes.

Twin Lakes were used for retaining ponds to stock the Little South. Men hauled 10-gallon cans of rainbow and German Brown fingerlings to the lakes on wagons. The lakes contained freshwater shrimp, a favorite food for fish, so they grew 7" a year. Alice could hardly wait to get over there and pull out 16-20" trout. After the fish reached a certain size, headgates were opened, allowing them to swim out into the river.

Until 1913, residents fished free with a six-month season. In 1921 the daily catch limit was 10 pounds of trout or grayling or

Fish caught by Alice. Dickerson photo.

20 pounds in possession and a minimum length of 7". Resident males over sixteen could fish for $1 from 1913-1917; Alice could fish free until 1939, because that was the law for women and young boys under sixteen. Most fish caught were natives and eastern brook trout averaging 10-12".

People came up from the valley in spring wagons. They cleaned the fish, salted them inside and hung them on a wire making sure they did not touch each other, thereby allowing them to dry before transporting them home. Fish were plentiful; sometimes riders on horseback dropped a line without even getting off and caught all they wanted, or were allowed.

Greeley fishermen home from the mountains. Charlie Matheson, unidentified person and Karl Bliss. Photo by Art Deffke about 1912.

The Sawmillers

The sawmill was a means of earning table beans
So the Dickerson men began it;
Trees were cut down, boards taken to town
And sold by the men who ran it.
An engine was sought which Sam and Earl bought--
Took six horses to pull it up there;
They cut lumber galore to help the war
But profit was small for their share.

Hauling lumber from the plains with which to build homes, barns and other outbuildings was highly impractical for homesteaders creating a lifestyle forty miles up in the mountains, especially when utilizing the only mode of transportation they had...horsepower. Power-driven machines for sawing logs into lumber, sawmills, were not only handy on-the-scene board-makers for settlers' own use, but they were a tool for creating a product to sell.

Ed Sherwood, who had homesteaded on Cascade Creek in the Buckhorn prior to the Dickersons, was the first to place a sawmill on the Dickerson ranch. He had brought it up to saw some timbers. It was a big steam engine that could be pulled from place to place, unlike small machines, and he had brought it up with a team. Sherwood, a prim New York school teacher, had sawed the lumber for the first two rooms of Sam's house. But, due to a heavy World War I demand for timber in 1918, Dickersons recognized a commercial potential and started a sawmill of their own.

They hauled up a sawmill and old steam engine which they had purchased from one of the Hyatts, who had then moved to Drake in the Big Thompson Canyon. Six horses were required to pull it up to the Dickerson place. The little girls were thrilled watching the horses towing the outfit past their house. The family cut lumber with it for many years before it finally expired.

Trees were cut with two-man saws, snaked out with teams of horses and brought to the mill. Allen, Sam and Earl worked at the sawmill so the family could acquire enough money to live on; they did not make much; just an existence.

Old Dickerson sawmill and Allen.   *Forest Service photo.*

The Trapper

At dawn she heard the call of a bird
And occasional scold of a squirrel;
The trapline trail over hills she'd scale
Kept the blood pumping fast in the girl;
With snow to her knees she'd trudge through the trees
Making trails like the wild things she sought;
Young Alice the girl was Nature's sweet pearl
In harmony with the creatures she caught.

While the men were working the sawmill and Helen was taking care of her bedridden grandmother, during the winter months Alice walked a 15-mile trap line for nine or ten years until furs were worthless. It was a means, for awhile, of earning a few badly-needed dollars. Through the years she caught over 50 coyotes, 50 bobcats, cross foxes, ermine, red foxes and civit cats. Most of this endeavor was during the depression years.

She started the trek from her home, up through Monument Gulch, back by the main road, halfway up Pennock Pass, back toward White Pine, down the Buckhorn, up on Sherwood Hill...all over the country. Sometimes, if someone else took care of Cora, Helen would go with her, even though she wasn't crazy about going. Alice would say, "Don't you want to go along?"and Helen would go with her. Sometimes her father would go with her; sometimes he would go by himself if Alice did not feel well.

Alice walked from seven to fifteen miles, depending on whether she caught something.

"If I caught something, my adrenalin was up and I walked the whole thing in one day," recalled Alice.

She started wearing trousers when she started trapping, even though she really didn't like them. She explained, "If you didn't wear trousers you might be up to your neck in snow. When Helen went with me, she wore them, too. I wore those felt boots like the Russians and cloth-topped overshoes. In the spring when it was wet sometimes they'd leak, but with dry snow they were warm and dry. I was outdoors most of the time even if I wasn't trapping. I didn't like long coats, so I had a short jacket I wore," said Alice.

Once her dad came up from the river and told her, "You got a skunk." Alice laughed. "Yes. I know. It fumed on you."

Alice was in Monument Gulch one morning checking traps.

The Trapper : Alice with bobcat.
Photo by Helen Dickerson, 1927.

She found a very fresh mountain lion track right on top of the trap. Another inch and he would have been caught. A little frightened, she decided to leave, but slipped on the ice and fell on her back. She got up as fast as she could and left swiftly, but did not run, as she had an uneasy feeling she was being watched.

Alice with two porcupines, in trousers and Russian boots.
Helen Dickerson photo, 1930s.

As with everything else on the homestead, nothing was easy and trapping was no exception. First she skinned the animal; then cased it, which meant stripping the hide before splitting it, and put it on a stretcher; then she let it dry. She sold the furs that way and buyers could "do whatever they pleased with them."

Alice, Helen and bobcats.   *Photo by Stella, 1930s.*

Alice remembered, "It was an awful job keeping the feet on. They wanted to make rugs out of them, so I tried to fix them that way, but it wasn't easy. I'd take two sticks and try to pull the tail out in one piece without breaking or splitting it. Took several days to dry them. And then in 1930 I only got $90 for the whole year. Like nothing."

The Dickerson sisters liked to relate a story about a man

illegally trapping for beaver up a gulch near Thompson's Resort, now Mishawaka, in the Poudre Canyon. "He reached for some leaves to cover his bear trap and caught his arm in someone else's bear trap that had been there a long time. Luckily he had his trap clamps or he would never have gotten out. After being in a bear trap himself, he said he would never trap again."

Across Pennock Pass Frank Koenig also trapped....fox, ermine, mink and lynx, and snowshoed on the Mummy to trap marten, selling his furs in the spring. Most winters in that country, if they needed to leave, Koenigs traveled on snowshoes, as there was too much snow for team and wagon.

The Twenties

Alice stayed up late in the year '28
  Listening to Admiral Byrd.
The Crosley was a gas hearing voices from o'er the pass
  The men were surprised at what they heard.
Some taps the girls changed so they were arranged
  To hear Bennett and Ford come in strong;
The men said, "My land, we can't understand
  How our coming you knew all along."

Men came from all around to Sam Dickerson's blacksmith shop on the homestead. Someone always needed work done, and Sam and Earl were as skilled as they came. They repaired many a wagon for neighbors through the years.

Blacksmith shop. Photo 1915, photographer unknown.

Earl had a tire shrinker; in dry weather the wheel wood shrank so the tire would come off the wheel. He wrapped the wheel in gunny sacks for water retention and soaked it in hot water; this fixed the wheel so the tire would stay on. They also had long bars of pig iron they could cut and shape for a new tire when the old ones were too thin to use anymore.

Sam setting a wagon wheel. Old Dickerson photo, early 1900s.

Horseshoeing was another major part of the blacksmith business. Most of the time it was fairly routine with gentle horses, but Sam and Earl dreaded it when horses came in from Pingree Park to be shod. Pingree Park had more than its share of locoweed, which sometimes made the animals so crazy they had to be killed. At best they were hard to put shoes on; they were too loco to shoe without throwing and tying them down, no easy chore for any men. At least the owner would stay and help the Dickersons handle them. They put a long heavy pole between the horse's legs, tied all four legs to it and then nailed on the shoes. It could and often did take all day to shoe four loco horses.

Stella was in Windsor with her father, who was dying of cancer, during part of 1920. The girls took over and boarded the Forest Service surveyors who were selecting a route for the telephone line over Pennock Pass.

In 1921 Dickersons saw their first deer, except the one dead in the snowdrift in 1913. The entire area was a game refuge all the way to the Poudre at that time. Refuges provided sanctuary for all animals except mountain lions and furbearers. The winter of 1921-22 was very severe, and in some portions of the state the Colorado Game & Fish Department officially fed wildlife.

Alice: "We had a horse worked baler a bit like this."

It was in the early 20s that Earl bought a hay baler from Ed Sherwood. It was horse operated; hay was hauled to it in a wagon and dropped into it with a pitchfork. Then a horse was led around and around working the plunger that pressed the hay into bales. A square hardwood block dropped between each bale of hay; then each was hand-tied with baling wire.

Some time between 1923 and 1925 the road from the Rockwell

Ranch to the Poudre Canyon was built. Crews used plows, scrapers with teams of horses, dynamite and all drilling was done by hand.

In about 1925, the first road along the Little South from the Lazy D, past the Rockwell Ranch to Bennett Creek, where it joined the High Drive to the Poudre, was completed, or almost so. When it was, in fact, completed, it meant that, for the first time, a road existed all the way from Pingree Park, past the Derby (Lazy D) and Rockwell Ranches to the Poudre. Earl was the handiest man around sharpening drills, plows and other blacksmithing jobs during construction of that section of the road. Alice went with Allen one day in his Model T Ford over Pennock Pass to the road crew camp by Pennock Creek. They had lunch with Earl and the crew and Alice remembered that they kept their meat in a big square wire mesh box hanging in a pine tree.

One of the most delightful additions to the Dickerson household in the late 20s was a little Crosley radio earphone set. Stella's brother owned a radio shop in Fort Collins, so he took the radio up to see if it worked at the remote homestead. He brought them four sets of earphones so, if they wanted, they could all listen at once. Though the reception was good, it whistled at every station. But the faraway stations came in better than the radios of the 1990s. They received Tennessee, Iowa and others too numerous to mention, and for the high country mountain folk, listening to that radio was a real treat. Calgary, Canada came in unbelievably clear. The little radio was the first set in that region of the mountains. Ranger Payson, however, had the first radio with a speaker.

Alice demonstrating the Crosley earphones. Photo by Elyse Bliss, 1993.

Alice loved listening to the radio and one night in 1928 she sat nestled under the earphones until 2 a.m. listening to Commander Richard Byrd talking from Little America in Antarctica. She was thrilled to hear him talking live from so far away.

The girls had a little fun with the radio one day. They were manipulating the little station-changing buttons, called "taps" and suddenly recognized voices they knew. The familiar voices were Mr. Ford from the Rockwell Ranch, Tom Bennett, Frank Koenig and Ranger Payson. They were conversing on their telephones about meeting at Dickersons to do some telephone line repairs, what tools they should bring and other interesting bits of local business. When the men all arrived the next day, they were baffled that the girls, who had no phone at that time, knew they were coming, until Alice told them what they had said on the radio. And they were still baffled about how that could happen. After they went home, the men tried to test the little technique on their radios, but to no avail; their radios were not the same type. Sometimes Alice and Helen changed taps and could hear familiar Poudre Canyon voices talking about selling cream, butter and eggs and other interesting topics in their telephone conversations.

Now that the entire road was finished from Pingree Park to the Poudre, the U.S. Forest Service and telephone company installed the telephone line to the Poudre. Just before Cora died in 1930, Allen bought a telephone from Fletchers at Livermore. It was a real milestone for the remote mountaineers; Dickersons had Livermore as Central via the Rockwell Ranch. Before they answered, they had to count the rings; theirs was four longs and a short. They had to pick up the receiver first to make certain nobody was on the line; then they could ring directly to another party. To get the operator, they rang one ring.

People from all around were intrigued with Lou Starkey, who had bought Hugh Ramsey's home in Pingree Park. He always seemed to be inventing something. He took an old car and stripped off everything it could run without. Then he attached log chains with cross pieces from front to back wheels like a caterpillar track. At his sawmill he made skis from boards and fastened them to his front axle, thereby making the first snowmobile anyone in those parts had ever seen. He used it when the snow was deep to get from Pennock Creek to Pingree Park and onlookers were in awe of their mechanical genius neighbor when they saw what he had invented. Later, in North Park, ranchers used a very similar rendition to take sleds of hay to stranded cattle. Starkey also invented the first "serve yourself" gas pump and patented it.

The Buckhorn Canyon contained a few illicit goings-on, about which, for protection of the innocent descendants, names are not mentioned. A still was operating and the stuff was ready to sell, but a neighbor spilled the beans and the bootleggers were sent to prison, threatening to kill the informant, if and when they were released. Things were a little tense for awhile, but as time went on, the fascinating events were practically forgotten.

A "rascal" who lived down the Buckhorn cut a man's throat, but he did not die, so the attacker was not prosecuted. Likely the same man was one of the notorious horse thieves; at least he was a prime suspect. Another young resident and a friend started to hold up a dance hall down at Masonville, but he accidentally stuck a candle instead of a shell into his shotgun. The attempt failed, due to the slip-up, but the boys escaped.

The Basketmaker

She practiced and practiced making pine needle baskets
While tending her grandma during rest:
Her first one was crude and Alice had booed,
"It looks like a magpie nest!"
But undaunted she wove, for success she strove
To make all her baskets pretty.
Soon everyone found her creations were sound
And they rushed up to buy from the city.

Cora had a stroke and was bedfast for eight years. Sam and the rest of the family were busy with other money-making endeavors, so Helen, twelve years old, took care of her grandmother during the day.

Helen stayed close so if her grandmother needed her she was available. In her spare time, she experimented with making a basket out of willow bark and pine needles. This gave her something to do during slack times on the long days. Alice teased her that her first one looked like a magpie nest, but at least it was a semblance of a basket. Not being easily discouraged, Helen kept practicing and eventually earned a little more respect from her older sister; she was, indeed, fashioning beautiful baskets from native plant life.

Helen and Sam with Cora in wheelchair. Date and photographer unknown.

She advanced from willow bark to cord, and continued with the mountain-grown pine needles, which were very short in length.

These she used for years. Never in her life had she even seen a pine needle basket; just got it in her head to make some. Helen became so proficient at basket-making that soon the word got around that little Helen Dickerson was making beautiful pine needle baskets, a real novelty.

On May 11, 1930, Cora Dickerson passed away and was buried in Windsor, Colorado. Now that "Grandma" was gone, six Dickersons were left to operate the many-faceted homestead.

"We really did live off the land," said Alice. "Lumber, posts, poles, baskets, trapping, venison, garden, wild berries, huckleberries, fish ... whatever we could find."

Cora Emma Dickerson 1858 - 1930.   Old Dickerson photo.

III.
THE REALLY LEAN YEARS
1930–1937

Gold Nugget and Golden Eagle

Alice slung hash and carried out trash
 At the Gold Nugget though meagerly paid;
Golden Eagle was busy making Helen 'bout dizzy
 Selling Mountain Delight and Maid;
She sent Alice candy and thought it'd be dandy
 If she sold some to tourists over there
Alice had intention, but to tourists didn't mention;
 She ate it all herself like a bear.

Shortly after Cora Dickerson died, Helen and her father built a stand alongside the road south of their cabin from which Helen could sell souvenirs, including her baskets that were becoming so popular. Helen named it the "Golden Eagle".

Helen at her Golden Eagle stand.
*Photo by Red Fenwick, **Denver Post**, 1954.*

She started out intending to sell just souvenirs, but when the Bockman timber camp came in over near Ballards' and the Hurley camp on top of Pennock Pass, soda pop, candy bars, cigarettes and other popular consumption items were in so much demand that she increased her inventory. She made only a pittance on those items as she charged just one or two cents over cost, but she did it only to please the "timber-whackers."

FRED MEYERS, Gen. Mgr.

FLAKS, INC.

Wholesale

DRUGS AND SUNDRIES

CIGARS, CIGARETTES, TOBACCO

CHEWING GUM AND CANDY

DISTRIBUTORS FOR

PARK & TILFORD CANDY,
ROCKY FORD, MURIEL AND TRAIN MASTER CIGARS

FLAKS BUILDING
1848-50 Arapahoe St.

DENVER, COLORADO

PHONE { KEystone 7403
{ KEystone 7406

Apr. 28th, 1931.

Miss Helen Dickerson,
Masonville, Colo.

Dear Madam:

We are in receipt of your order which has received our prompt attention, and for which we thank you.

Wish to advise that our price on 5¢ Candy Bars is $.75 per box, net, and our price on Gums is $.57 per box, net.

Trusting that this is the information that you desire, and hoping that we may be favored with more orders in the future, we are

Very truly yours,

Alice was not at home the summer the stand was built. Bennetts came across the pass to get her in May so she could work at their Gold Nugget tourist resort, which later became Sky Ranch, at Hourglass Lake. She worked all summer slinging hash and doing everything else required of her by her bosses.

Bennett had come from England originally to escape the fog and smoke. He had tuberculosis and lived on the Tom Gard homestead, which he purchased, for a number of years before returning to England for his bride. Mrs. Bennett, in her riding skirt, charmed everyone by riding sidesaddle. Tom had built the original White Pine Tower from 1913-1918. He also built a winter home on the homestead and moved to the Gold Nugget May through September.

Most of the tourists were from the east and stayed several weeks; some even stayed all summer. Tourists loved being met by

*A Party on the Way to Hague's Peak
on the Mummy Pass Trail*

The Bennett Ranch

IN THE HEART OF THE ROCKIES

COMANCHE LODGE
EGGERS, COLORADO
Larimer County

Do you want to sit by the hour in brilliant sunshine a roaring waterfall or in fragrant pine woods; to sleep long nights beyond the reach of all sound except the bark of a far off coyote or the bell of a grazing cow or horse; to meet a few persons of tastes like your own but to be perfectly independent of them should you choose?

Do you wish for a time to give up a few luxuries for more freedom? To live at a higher level and slower pace? To feel the kinks disappear from your mind and muscles as you ride up to timber line to cook your lunch almost in a snow bank and fish in a solitary lake? Or to know the joy of letting a horse carry you over a steep, flower bordered trail, fording streams as you must and glorying in the unspeakable beauty of forest and mountains?

One of the Many Beautiful 1

Our ranch can offer you these opportunities. It is in northern Colorado about fifty-six miles from the City of Fort Collins by way of Poudre Canon and Bennett Creek Roads and forty-six miles from the City of Loveland by way of Masonville and the Buckhorn Road, and is off the beaten track of tourists away from any main road which might mean possible annoyance from stragglers; is safe from intruders, and yet accessible by motor stage from Fort Collins, by your own car, or we meet trains at Loveland or Fort Collins.

Comanche Lodge is our guest house. It has a living room with fireplace and bed rooms; some of them more like sleeping porches, but protected from occasional showers and offering as much privacy as the rooms. There is a bath in the lodge with hot and cold water. The lodge is about one hundred yards from the ranch house, where all meals are served.

In the woods near the house you can find some of the blue Colorado Columbines, and a part of the pasture is blue with a species of fringed gentian which never fails to appear in the same place.

For fishermen—and we find there are successful enthusiasts of both sexes—there is Big Beaver Creek up which you may fish for miles, or well stocked lakes for our own guests.

When you wish to try the longer and more difficult trails, a guide will go with you at reasonable rate. You can ride through tall timber along Beaver Creek trail to timber line and Mummy Range from which you look over to the Continental Divide, and pick Columbines and Alpine Primroses at an altitude of nearly 12,000 feet. You will certainly want to go to the Mummy Pass, where you may expect to get a glimpse of the shy ptarmigan quail and possibly of the rare Rocky Mountain sheep. Trips can also be taken to Comanche Mountain, 13,000 feet, Hague's Peak and Hallett's Glacier, 13,500 feet, and numerous other government trails.

If you do not know how to ride you can learn on a sure-footed, reliable horse.

You will need few real summer clothes and may live all day in riding clothes if you choose. Do not forget to bring one or two woolen shirts, a slicker, some warm underwear and sweater. You will have plenty of use for your camera and will enjoy field glasses if you have them.

Trout Lakes Near the Ranch

Although the ranch is a place for rest, it is not a health resort. We do not take persons who have lung trouble or any form of communicable disease. It is also in your own interest, as well as that of other guests, that we ask for references from strangers.

A Rest on the Continental Divide

ALSO CABINS FOR RENT

Our rates are reasonable and for particulars concerning them or any other detail about which you wish to know please write Mr. and Mrs. Thomas P. Bennett & Son, Comanche Lodge, Eggers, Larimer County, Colorado. Telephone Livermore exchange No. 10-F13.

Be sure to allow time for possible delay in our receiving or sending letters before the summer mail schedule starts on June first.

OUR REFERENCES:

MR. CLEVELAND R. CROSS
MIDLAND BANK BUILDING
CLEVELAND, OHIO

MR. DON VICK ROY
1502 SPEER BOULEVARD
DENVER, COLORADO

MRS. WM. MORRIS DAVIS
CALIFORNIA

MISS L. M. HOLMES
25 WESTBOURNE TERRACE
BROOKLINE, MASSACHUSETTS

MISS G. SHERIFF
3266 PARKWOOD AVENUE
TOLEDO, OHIO

DR. J. G. McFADDEN
LARIMER COUNTY
LOVELAND, COLORADO

FIRST NATIONAL BANK
LARIMER COUNTY
LOVELAND, COLORADO

MISS M. E. COOK
105 CENTRE STREET
MILTON, MASSACHUSETTS

Tom Bennett either in Loveland or Ft. Collins and brought up to the resort in a spring wagon drawn by a team of mules.

This was early in the Depression and Colorado did not yet have a serious problem with lack of tourism. In fact, tourism held up through 1930 because of lodging in new cottage camps and low gasoline prices. This scenario did not hurt Helen with her new stand; passersby were becoming more commonplace.

While Alice was at the Gold Nugget, she heard about the little stand Helen and Earl had built and about the candy Helen was selling. Helen made her own candy called Mountain Delight and Mountain Maid, which everyone was raving about. Alice asked her to send her some, thinking she could sell it to tourists at the Nugget. But...it was so good, Alice ate most of it.

Alice got sick in September, not from eating Helen's candy, but from overwork.

"They worked me almost to death," Alice said, "I was so thin, I looked like a snake." She returned home to recuperate and help the family.

Dickerson Guest Cabin

The Dickerson ladies had become the darlings of the entire Mummy Range area. Work crews, rangers and many others either ate meals in the Dickerson home or rented their guest cabin and boarded there. When the work crew from Lyons combined Lily and West Lakes to make Comanche Reservoir, they stopped often at the stand for hamburgers, coffee and home-made candy bars, which Helen continued to make for several years. Alice was home by the time the crew got caught one fall day in a heavy snowstorm

95

and had to quit working. The first thing the men thought of was, "Call Dickersons", so they called from Bennetts' and asked the ladies to have a hot lunch for them; they were comin' over the mountain if they could make it. When the several carloads joyfully arrived, they came to the door singing, "When It's Springtime in the Rockies" and they happily stuffed themselves on beans, fresh homemade bread and coffee.

Helen's stand.

Stormy Weather

Black Blizzards brought dust, which everyone cussed;
*   The snow turned pink as a rose.*
They still cut ice, a job not nice--
*   Sawed it by hand and 'bout froze.*
The old mill was done so they bought another one;
*   It came on its own steam power.*
The whistle on a curve made a car jump and swerve
*   And the driver cussed Allen with a glower.*

In eastern Colorado four years of drouth began in 1931. The dryland farmers had been exposing their fields to the hot, dry winds by excessive plowing ever since World War I. With nothing growing, "Black Blizzards" could pick up the exposed topsoil and carry it great distances, where it would darken the skies and drift down to the ground. The Dickerson homestead was no exception. One April the sky appeared like a heavy fog drifting in from the east before a wet snow fell. The snow was so red Alice brought some into the house to melt. She ended up with a thick layer of fine, red mud, like talc, in the bottom of a jar. After several spring storms, the snows covering the mountain soil returned to normal.

Alice continued trapping during the winter months. Before she bought her first car, Allen took some of her furs to Ft. Collins in his Ford. She packaged others and mailed them from Masonville to a Denver fur dealer, Harry Amann. She ended her full-time

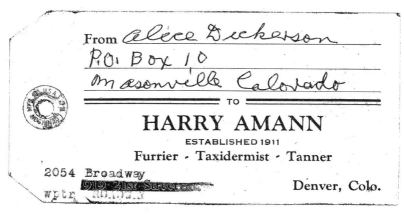

trapping by having a coat made from six coyote hides. She did not sell them, because they were worth almost nothing—$2 each.

On the trail ;
Alice with
bobcat.
Helen Dickerson
photo, 1930s.

Alice later gave the coat to Cecil Summers. She continued trapping off and on throughout the thirties, but with less and less zeal.

Alice also continued helping her dad get ice, one of their most miserable winter chores. They had to cut it by hand and about froze to death. It had to be real cold, or the ice would "honeycomb" and be rotten. Once Alice thought her father was going to be killed when they had a load of ice on the wagon. He went around a post, awfully close, and if the horses had not stopped, he would have been crushed by a wagon wheel.

Meanwhile, the day-to-day work went on. Road crewmen widening the Pennock Pass road, though staying both in the log ranger station and in tents nearby, were boarding with Stella. Earl and Allen worked with them, too. It was the first road work done around the area with dozers and tractors, but they also used teams.

Truck hauling Forest Service boys to work widening Pennock Pass.
Photo by Alan Dakan, 1930s.

Widening the pass.   *Photo by Dakan, 1930s.*

One day after a big spring snow the Dickersons were surprised to see a woman approaching from Pennock Pass on snowshoes. As the woman got closer, they recognized Mrs. Koenig. She told them she was going to Loveland, so she spent the first night at Dickersons'. The next night she spent with the Simpsons just beyond the Stove Prairie road and several places after that. That

was a long way to walk on snowshoes...close to 40 miles!

The old sawmill finally wore out and they bought another one from Roy Hyatt. This one was a big steam engine which had been used for threshing grain. Allen drove it up under its own power. While he was en route, a car came around a curve and the driver honked impatiently. Not to be outdone, Allen steered the monstrous machine out of the way and casually pulled the whistle, which closely resembled that of a railroad engine. The startled driver almost plunged into the creek, closely followed by a frenzied attempt to gain control of the auto and coupled with not just a few choice words emitted from the open window of the car. As Alice put it, "He about jumped over himself." Allen placed the newly-acquired machine near the garden and once again they

Alice: "We had a tractor engine like this for sawmilling."

100

Allen at the sawmill.
Forest Service photo.

were in business.

When they weren't working on the road, Sam, Earl and Allen were sawmilling and Sam and Earl were blacksmithing. Allen never darkened the doorstep of the blacksmith shop; he was strictly a sawmiller. Occasionally a deadbeat took advantage of the sawmillers. Alice and Earl hauled a wagon load of lumber to a gold-mining shack up the draw from the Deadman schoolhouse. Prospectors' holes dotted Deadman Hill, suspected by the Dickersons to be a promotor's scheme, as no gold reportedly was ever found. What mattered, though, to Alice and her father was that they did not get paid.

As if the worst Depression years, 1932-1936, were not bad enough for the Colorado farmers, the grasshopper depredation made them markedly worse. The Agricultural Experiment Station of the Colorado Agricultural College in Fort Collins in 1917 and subsequent years published bulletins telling farmers how to deal with the problem. Farmers went up to the Dickerson sawmill, got truckloads of sawdust, took it down to Greeley and mixed it with molasses, Paris green and bran for poison. Allen was glad to give sawdust to them, as he always had a problem disposing of it. The farmers told the Dickersons that the grasshoppers were so thick that even cars on the road were sliding on them and that people could hardly go outdoors without them hopping into their faces. Of course, the worst problem was that they were eating their crops down to the soil.

Shed in which was mixed by hand a large quantity of Paris green-bran mash during the grasshopper campaign, 1916. **Grasshopper Control Bulletin #233,** *June 1917. Agricultural Experiment Station, Colorado Agricultural College.*

A hopper dozer in action in war against grasshoppers, 1916. Photo by Agricultural Experiment Station, Colorado Agricultural College.

102

People will say that kerosene will not freeze, but Dickersons discovered that is not true. One day it was -40° and they started to put some kerosene in a lamp and found it had ice on top; they could scrape it off with their fingers.

At the other extreme, on a warm summer day, a thunderstorm came up in the afternoon. Earl, Helen and Allen ran into the kitchen to escape the rain. Alice and Stella were in Windsor. Helen had her hands in the dishwater on the stove when suddenly a ball of fire about the size of a softball came down the chimney, just missed Helen and went down the sink. It had hit a tree behind the house. When they recovered from the shock and surveyed the damage, the lightning bolt had gone through cans of gasoline, spilling the gas, killed a litter of kittens and burned a hole in a carpenter's square, making it look like it had been soldered. It had been a violent storm with torrents of rain and Alice and Stella had trouble getting home.

The Craft Creators

Long winter nights with very dim lights
Brought beautiful creations all new;
Baskets and clocks and freshly-darned socks
Were accomplished to name just a few.
Painting and tatting, salt beads and quilt batting
Were most always made after day;
Aladdin was glowing and customers were knowing
That the stand would be open in May.

The Dickerson crafts had become a tourist attraction and it became an all-consuming job for the girls, especially Helen, who made baskets summer and winter to keep up. Helen's baskets were in much demand and Alice made toothpick holders and paintings. Helen also made bolo ties from antlers and Alice painted on them.

The ties were hard work; Helen had to drill holes, put screws in them, then glue. Alice began making beautiful and unique collages depicting landscapes with rustic cabins, fences, trees and animals.

The girls went to Geiger's homestead in Deadman Canyon to cut some cedar logs and hauled them to Allen so he could cut their boards for the bases of Helen's baskets. Then they started making clocks of

Second collage created by Alice.
Photo by Elyse Bliss, 1993.

104

cedar and aspen in flower and wildlife shapes. They were too difficult and time-consuming to make, however, so they gave that up. For many years afterwards people brought others to look at the clocks and were disappointed there weren't any. But every spring, with or without clocks, they had big boxes of crafts ready to transport to the stand. People knew that; after a long, cold winter, instinctively they knew that the Dickerson women would have fresh treasures to sell and they came from every direction to see and buy the new creations.

Helen inside Golden Eagle.   *Photo by Red Fenwick,* **Denver Post**, *1954.*

Stella made rag rugs, as did many of the other homesteaders' wives. She patched, tatted, embroidered, painted pictures and made salt beads for necklaces. Salt beads were made out of salt and flour, then solidified with glue and dyed. Some women made men's watch chains out of horse tail hair. Stella did not have much time for those things, including her painting, because she had too much else to do. But what she did have time to make always exhibited her natural talent. She always told her daughters she would paint during her old age.

The house was lighted with an Aladdin coal oil mantle lamp. It made a very good light, which Stella, Alice and Helen badly needed for their craft-making during the long winter nights. The lamp had to be watched carefully, however; the mantle would get black if the air was not right. Changes in the air produced changes in its burning velocity. If the family ran out of coal oil they had to open the door of the heating stove and see by burning woodlight. The #2 burner lamps which the Dickersons utilized earlier did not make a very good light by which to read and work. They tried to always have candles in reserve so they could see to cook supper in case they ran out of lamp fuel. Often they just went to bed at dark because they could not see.

Painting by Stella Dickerson.

Later Critters

Anyone would want to see a dog toting milk to be
A mama to a calf down at the barn;
A tomato growing on a vine before the frost prevents a dine
Or meat in a pan from a steer who wouldn't larn.
Alice decided to get a pig, brought home two not so big;
They grew up bigger than the donor had.
A bum lamb bonked a board, a greedy deed it couldn't afford
'Cause Alice used him for trapping bait, poor lad!

The dairy chores continued right on through the Depression. Helen had trained their English Shepherd dog to carry a 5 or 6-lb. bucket of milk from the house to the barn. She gave the milk to the calf and it would lick the dog's nose, or vice versa. It even tried to suck the dog's nose. He was a good cattle dog and a Dickerson family member for seventeen years. One day he turned up missing and Alice found him in one of her coyote traps, but not badly hurt. Another time she ran over him, but fortunately he was behind the car where chickens had been dusting or he would have been killed.

Joe with milk bucket.   *Helen Dickerson photo, early 30s.*

Helen had become accustomed to going to get the cows as part of her daily routine. One day she caught a glimpse of two steers slipping like elk through the lodgepoles. Not just a little surprised, she kept an eye out for them and discovered they were

Joe bringing milk to calf.   *Helen Dickerson photo, early 30s.*

hanging out near her milk cows. Finally she saw them long enough to read the brand, the Box S. Knowing that brand belonged to the Maitland Ranch around Miller's Fork, she wrote to them. Maitlands were very surprised, because they had not seen the steers since they had turned them out on the range five years before when they were little calves. They came many times trying to catch them, but left each time having caught only a fleeting glimpse of the elusive critters, if that. At long last, on a very foggy day, the cowboys succeeded in driving the elusive steers to the Ballard place and thought at last they had them. But the aggravating critters slipped away and one man even disappeared. Next day they came with their truck and 30-30 rifle and found their fog-bound man comfortably warm in the Ballard cabin. This time when they found the steers they ended up "hog-dressing" them behind the Dickerson barn. That meant taking the entrails out, leaving the hide on and legs up in the air so the meat would not get dirty. Then they took them to market. They were big steers, so they had fared well in the high Rocky Mountain wild.

Alice detested livestock, but it was one of the necessities of life on the homestead so she, of course, helped. They raised at different times cows, pigs, chickens, rabbits, a few sheep and kept cats and dogs for friends. One time when the girls were visiting their uncle in Windsor he was planning to kill some of his sixteen pigs because there were too many to eat at their mother's feeding stations. He gave Alice two of the smallest ones and, after feeding them for several months, she ended up with larger pigs than his. He was, being a seasoned farmer, impressed.

A friend down on the Buckhorn had a bunch of extra or orphaned lambs, called "bums". Alice and Helen took home seven and bottle-fed them three times a day. The girls kept them in a big pen so they would not have predator trouble. One eager little lamb was so greedy it knocked itself out when it crashed into a board trying to get a bottle. It later became sick and died. Alice used it for trapping bait and caught a fox and a bobcat. Indirectly that lamb brought more money, sixteen dollars, than if she had sold it as a live sheep. A visiting city cousin, when watching Alice administering castor oil to one of the lambs, asked her if the lamb had done something wrong.

"Why, no," said Alice. "What makes you think that?"

"Well," said cousin Shirley, "my mother always gave me castor oil when I was bad."

Down in the Valley

Alice left home, an excuse to roam
At the request of her uncle T.G.;
He thought it'd be nice if she'd care for his wife
Who was sick as she could be.
So to Windsor she went and six months spent
And she bought her very first car;
She learned how to drive, enough to survive
When driving her coupe very far.

Helen never wanted to go anyplace; she was perfectly content to stay at home and pursue her many interests. But Alice had a deep desire to leave the nest and see the world outside. Thus, when her uncle, T.G. Foster of Windsor, came up one day in the fall of 1931 and asked her if she would come down to take care of his sick wife, Alice was packed and almost ready to go before he had finished his first cup of Postum. She had recovered from her illness after leaving Bennetts' the previous fall and felt fit as a fiddle.

It did not take Stella long after Alice left to begin writing letters. Excerpts:

Eggers, Colo
9-23-31

Dear Alice:

Well I wonder if you are having a good time and if you have been looking for a car yet. Well don't get one unless you want to, it may be as you say you may want your money for something else. It is hard to tell what may turn up to need it for.

We heard yesterday that the big Bank of England had closed its doors and that may affect the U.S. although Hoover says not.

The fellow who brought the other tomatoes brought us a bushel more last night from below Masonville. They are lovely ones and cost 50¢.

Some drunks wakened us about four oclock Monday morning. They were sure honking their horn at the stand. Daddy went down there and they wanted gas they said. (Will tell you more about that when you come home).

Love to all,
Mother

In September, Sam and Allen went to Ohio to visit old friends and relatives, so the old homestead that fall was missing a few of its inhabitants for awhile. The men also sent an occasional message as they chugged along to and in Ohio.

9-25-31
Peoria, Ill

Dearest Family,
   We are some where near Indiana but don't know where. Made 270 miles yesterday. We bought 25 cents stock in the Miss river
                        S D D

T.G.'s wife got well in a short time under Alice's care, but instead of going home, Alice decided to stay and work. This was indeed a real adventure for her. She kept house for a local doctor and his family that winter. She remained with her aunt and uncle for awhile, but eventually moved in with the people for whom she worked, because she did not want to disrupt her relatives all the time when she left early for work. Later she lived with people who worked at the Windsor Post Office.

Correspondence from Alice's family continued throughout the winter: Excerpts:

10-4-31
My dear girl,
   Why haven't you written me at least one card if you didn't have time to write a letter. Pop has been doing some work on cattle gard. Pat to come over tomorrow and he and Daddy finish it together. Pop went down last Monday and stayed all night at Roswells. About six dollars worth of tobacco was taken from the stand and some gas from truck that night. Don't know who got it but are not telling it all around so perhaps we can trace who got it better so don't tell this out side or tell the folks not to tell any one yet at least if you tell them.
   Mr. Gray moved his family in our house at Masonville.

                        With love,
                        Mom

10-6-31

   Alice if you haven't bought a car and want to come home if someone can bring you to Masonville you can find a chance to come up soon I think with either Roswell or Kitchen. Did Edwin get that grain for Pop? Mr. Roswell was coming up after some wood this week and Kitchen after more props. Guess there is no rush about your coming if you want to stay longer but would like to hear from you any way. If come to Masonville could probably stay at Kitchens or Roswells. Alice if get a chance get a quart of Wesson oil or any other that is good for salad oil. We want some to mix with some peanut butter.

If they have open season on Elk first part of Nov. Payson said he wanted to get one and if he did he would divide with us.

Those people who got Helens tobacco took the pop bottles off in front of stand but left bottles down the road a little way. (Guess they didn't like the brand.) Ha Ha.

Mom

10-10-31

Dear Alice:
We are getting along all right. Pop has not been out after provisions. He and Pat have been working on the cattle gard all week are nearly done. As soon as Turner gets some logs in Orr Rockwell and Pop plan to saw. Don't know when he can get out to get the grain. When we had a little snow storm the other day he thought he had better leave the work and go after it but he hates to let a chance to make some money slip and the snow melted during the day.

We don't know who got in the stand. They slid the glass window up and reached in from there.

You didn't tell us what kind of car you got. Is it a Coupe or Roadster and what make and where did you get it. What kind of work are you doing and where are you working. And don't you want a few of your clothes that are here such as slips, bloomers, hose and house dress and brown hat.

Got a letter from Grandpa. They got there all right, had three flat tires. He said it didn't look like he thought it would there and he thought they would be back before long didn't know when.

Helen still has some business. She was counting up yesterday and has taken in $200 this summer but a great deal has been spent again. Not so bad though is it and she enjoys it. Sold nearly 600 bars homemade candy.

Love to all,
Mom

10-18-31
Roscoe, Ohio

Dear Helen and Alice

    There were 25 or 30 men asked for a ride, but we were hard boiled and did not take them in. There was two wemon asked for a ride. We were awful sorry for them and did not take them in. They only wanted to go to Columbus about 35 miles and a good road so we let them walk. Poor girls. I don't like Ohio would not want to stay here.

          Yours as ever,
          Grand Pa

10-28-31

Dear Earl and Family,

    What's the matter with you why don't you write us. Hope you are all well. what kind of wether are you having up there?

    They all ask about Earl and the girl that kills bob cats also a bout helen and stela. Dwight and Grace went up in an airplain while we were up at Ikes. they said it was fine he can tell you more about it when we get home. wish the girls had of come with us I no they would of had a good time.

          Yours,
          Father S.D.Dickerson

11-2-31

Dear Alice-

    I really haven't any thing to say but will shake this pen over the paper a little.

    There were five folks here half a day yesterday. They had two flat tires up the pass and the two men walked down to get some patchings and pump but we had no patchings or at least not here. it was in the truck and the truck wasn't here. We had the old pump of Sherwoods but the pump didn't help much without the patches and every one they stopped either didn't have any thing or just pump so we had a real nice visit with them till the truck got here at about sun down. There were two men two women and a little girl and they were from Missouri. They have a saw mill in Bennett Creek.

    Now for where the truck was. Mr. Roswell came up Saturday to take it for some gass. Pop and Moffet were cutting logs so I went up to help him get it ready. He put in the gass and the watter and the battery is run down and he said if I would take the rocks from the wheal he would stear it out in the sun where it would be easyer to pump the tires and start it so I got one rock out and couldn't get the other so I pushed it over it and there were no brakes in it and the farther it went the faster it went. his cow was back of the barn and he just did miss hitting it and the barn but he crawled between them and got it started up the hill then it stopped. then we filled the tires and cranked it for an hour more or less and finaly got it started but didn't get the brakes fixed and he didnd know how to work the gun so we got Moffet to go with him so between the two of them they went down and back not in one day tho.

I'm not in any hurry to come down so don't rush back on my acount. think I will keep the stand open for a few more weeks unless it snows so no body goes along.

Good by for now
Helen

12-29-31

Dear Alice:
Pop is putting up ice. it is very nice ice too. he had to come after his ice creepers just now as had been snowing just enough to make it slipery.

Helen and I took some pictures and printed some lovely postal cards Christmas day and evening. We had the best luck yet. We found out how to make a nice white margin on our cards.

We had a very good dinner if was only the three of us to eat it. We missed you a lot. It was the first Christmas you were ever away from us. Grandpa and Allen went to Denver for Christmas.

You will be surprised to hear that some of the teachers from the Agricultural College of Collins came clear up here and bought a blue kitten. We got 50¢ for it. That beats any way yet of disposing of them.

With love,
Mom

2-2-32

Dear Elsie, Alice & all:
I have not had any word since a letter you wrote the 25th Alice. Allen and Grandpa went down last week. If had not been for Kitchen coming along and pulling them out of the ice they would have been there quite a while as they were sure stuck. They had worked quite a while before Kitchen came. That place is below Sherwood hill where road was washed so bad in that last big wash out. The creek has backed up till it comes out into the road.

The wind has been terrible. It took our radio wire down last week but Earl got it fixed up better than before. Put on the new ariel

114

and stations come clearer than before. Cows are coming fresh have six new calves. Alice our goose gets so mean to the hens I don't know whether can make him behave so can keep him till Easter or not. I have enjoyed his noise he is a novelty to have around but had hoped you could at least come home for Easter and would eat him. Easter is last of March. The road is not fit for you to travel now.

Love,
Stella

2-16-32

Dear Alice

    I have had no luck trapping since I wrote to you. Not even a mouce. I did see one track yesterday. I think it was a fox.

    Mr. McCracin was back to see us last Sunday. He comes about once a week. He said he is going to get butter here now. So now he will have an excuse to stop at the house. It seems he likes to have one.

    We made a few more post cards last night. I made a cigarette show case a while back. Also a post card rack that will hold anyway 7 doz. cards & painted it black so they look real nice in it. I also want to try my luck at furniture making. Do you think I will do it.

Well good night,
Helen

2-17-32

    I don't know whether you could get home or not if you wanted to Alice. The men do get through occasionally.

    Suppose you are working for the postmistress by now. <u>Do you stay with her or Elsie at night</u>. I underscored this because I thought you might answer it better than you do some of my questions.

    Helen and I have been sewing some this week. We dyed some sacks pale green and orange to put some quilts together with. Used green and a brownish orange edge. It is quite pretty.

Love to all,
Mom

2-19-32

    Helen and I dressed our goose today he was so mean to the hens he killed one. He weighed 10½ pounds with the feathers and head off. I wish you were here to help eat it. Wish we could have kept it so Jinks' family and Edwin's could have come up to dinner when we ate

115

it, but I couldn't let him eat my hens. The hens are laying some. Have what we need to use.

Love
Mom

3-6-32

My dear girl:
Mrs. Roswell is making a pretty quilt. It is called the flower garden. It is cut out blocks in hexigon shape sewed in circles. She says the ladies down there have gotten up a club and they want all the Buckhorn ladies to attend. They only meet once a month and it is not a dress up club. They are to come in their house dresses. She wants us to come if we can. Helen made a cute pillow this week. She apliqueyed a little brown and white dog and moon on blue. She made a very nice rustic set of furniture last week of a board for seats and jack pines for legs and the rest. She made three chairs and a settee.

Those hooked rugs are very pretty. I have a machine to do it with and at least one needle. I had three but don't know where the others are. There are five beautiful patterns for hooked rugs in colors in our last "Womens World". I signed for it and "Pathfinder" and "Home Life". Got the three for $1.15 for a year's subscription. I also subscribed for the "Christian Herald" for two years. I am glad you have been going to church. Do you go alone?

I hope you will always have God as your guide and you know we can not know His will unless we study His Word.

Mr. McCracin is waiting for me to finish this to take it.

He said he would bring our mail back to us when he comes back.

Love to all,
Mom

3-6-32

Dear Alice
When you come home you will be trying to press the buttons for electricity, keep irons hot with out heating them on the stove, etc.

Did I tell you about how the bobcat I caught startled me when I first saw him. He was in the traps where you caught that pretty coyote last year and I walked up the road past them and on to the last set with out seeing any thing. But the birds had goten in some of the traps at the last set so when I came back I went over to the log where this set was, not thinking much about it, as I couldn't see anything from the road when I went up so didn't even look that direction till

116

I was by the log and on the other side was some yellow hair. I at first thought that don't look right then it got up and was a very angry kind of bait. Joe (dog) was with me too but he didn't tell me there was something there. He stays right at my heels and enjoys it a lot but he did a lot of squeaking when it got to jumping around and didn't want me to go any closer so I layed my gloves down and told him to stay with them so he did.

I am invited to a Social Club gathering at Stills place but don't suppose Allen will be going down just then.

MeCracin didn't get over last night or to night guess he thinks it is to cold. Yesterday we had a terrible cold blizzard and today it is cold and snowing. Grandpa told me last night it would be a bad night for By Crackey as he calls him.

I sat up till after midnight to hear the returns of the Lindburgh baby hunt that they was going to give but didn't hear anything but they didn't find him any way.

Lots of love,
Helen

3-12-32

Alice is there anything here of yours that you need? I have not heard from you for some time but there may be a letter at the store for us. We have not had our mail for quite awhile.

We have had quite a snow was about 16 or 18". Grandpa said it was 12 below when he looked at the thermometer and the sun was shining on it. Helen has been embroidering pillows. She made one for the lounge and one for your car. It is green velvet with a dog on it to keep hoodoos out (Ha Ha).

Allen may go down if he can get down tomorrow. He hasn't had a letter for some time. I am planning on putting peas all over the garden wherever that weed is the worst. There are places where it is not as bad as others so will put some garden for home mostly there. I believe we will have a wet summer and if do the peas would kill the weed where they are then could change about another year if we are still making garden by that time.

We have been listening to the news over radio every night. It is too bad for the Lindberghs about their little one being kidnapped. I feel so sorry for her as she is to have another in May which makes it all the worse.

I must make out some butter to send out. Only get 20¢ for it. Write soon. Do you have any place to keep your car, Alice.

With love,
Mom

117

3-19-32

Dear Alice
*   We would be glad if you could be home but don't try to start without telephoning Allen first and finding out when he is coming down and how the roads are. You could tell him when you wanted to start home and maybe he would go to Masonville to meet you.*

Love
Mom

5-21-32

Dear Alice:
*   I wonder why I have not heard from you lately. The last letter I had from you was dated the seventh. like one once a week at least.*
*   Helen had Mr. Kitchen bring up 50 gallons of gas. She ordered it before we got your letter. She thought you were coming home and would use part of it in your car. She thought she would have part of it to accomodate people who would stop for gas.*
*   Pop is all through with crops but at Station. He plowed there all day yesterday. He came home last night just drenched with water and mud to his knees. He said the ground was hard and he just kept turning it over. Has been disked the last few years.*
Love
Mom

In June Alice gave notice to all that she was quitting.

"I didn't just up and leave, which wouldn't have been very nice. They didn't want me to go back home, but I didn't want to stay there anymore; it was too hot," recalled Alice.

While she was in Windsor she bought her first car...a 1928 Plymouth coupe...with some of her "fur money" ($80) she had saved from trapping. She had learned how to drive that winter and felt a new sense of independence with the little car.

5-23-32

Dear Alice:
*   As I can send a letter out by Mrs. Kitchen this afternoon will write to you now. Get Helen 50¢ worth of one cent stamps for postal cards please.*
*   We are all glad you are planning on coming home next week. You won't need quite so much money to spend on your car up here as you won't be making very many trips and there is plenty to keep*

us entertained and busy also here in the summer.

Helen had quite a bit of business at the stand yesterday for this time of year. She is up finishing getting the cabin ready to rent. She thinks some one will want it when fishing season opens which is this week.

Perhaps you can make some money right here. You may be busy running the little saw don't know for sure yet.

Hope to see you soon.

Love
Mom

Alice drove to the coolness of her high-altitude home rejuvenated and knowing they needed her help up there. It was the last time Alice ever wanted to live down in the valley. She kept the letters her family had sent her that year; after all, they were the only letters her family had ever sent to her, because it was the only time she was ever gone for any length of time.

Stacks of Sacks

She crossed Pennock Pass with plenty of gas
And drove to the Eggers P.O.;
Mailbags just bulging—no time for indulging
In fishing or picnic or beau.
Helen rode along so if something went wrong
She could help sister Alice get through.
At the ranger's gate the CCCs would wait
For a letter from home—maybe two!

Alice stayed home, helped the family and now at least could drive to Fort Collins, Windsor or wherever if she wanted or needed to go. She used the little coupe in winter, too. Sometimes she had an awful time going to town because they did not clean out the road.

"You either did it yourself or you stayed home," Restless Alice said, and you could bet when she went out the door, she had shovel in hand, planning to, in fact, do it herself.

One day she and Helen did not get to town until 3:00 p.m. after having left at the crack of dawn. Earl and Stella, who at that time still had the telephone, a "hand grinder", called Mrs. Thompson at the Masonville Post Office and asked her to waylay the girls...not to let them come home that bitterly cold night. They were afraid they would get stuck and freeze to death because the snow had filled in their tracks and the road, which was really only two ruts, had become a terrible mess, even worse than it was when they went down. After a couple of days the girls got home safely, and Alice was becoming quite a seasoned driver in a hurry.

The U.S. Mail route for the Upper Buckhorn and Pingree Park area was from the U.S. Forest Service Ranger Station to Mr. Eggers' Post Office in the Poudre Canyon. Ben Scott was the first carrier and Mrs. Helen Payson, wife of Ranger Henry Payson, was the second. Paysons lived at the ranger station from 1924 until 1933.

Alice and Helen Payson became good friends and after Helen got tired of doing nothing and acquired the mail contract, Alice liked to go along with her. They were close in age, about 24, and liked to do things and go places together. They went to locations around the area like North Park, Glendevey, Fort Collins and even

dressed alike sometimes. They watched with interest the goings-on at the timber camp at Bennett Creek. Before the road turned to Crown Point there were a lot of houses, a schoolhouse and a steam-powered sawmill enclosed in rock and cement. The place was always alive with activity.

Ben Scott, first Upper Buckhorn mail carrier. Helen Dickerson photo, 1930.

"I was a gadabout," Alice reminisced, "I just wanted to wander, and so did Helen Payson. We had lots of fun. I still do like to wander." (1993 quote!)

Mrs. Payson ran the route for at least one term and had three months to go on her contract when her husband was transferred in 1933 and they had to move. Alice underbid everyone so she could finish the Payson contract. The wanderlust victim did not want to stay around home all the time, so the mail route was at least something. The pay was not all that great, but for Alice it was a welcome diversion in the summer months and she enjoyed it.

Alice Dickerson and Helen Payson. Helen Dickerson photo, 1930s.

Alice began her postal route in her little 1928 Plymouth coupe. Her working days were Tuesdays, Wednesdays and Saturdays from June through September. And if the 4th of July fell on one of those days, it was no holiday for Alice; the mail still went through.

Helen went with her sister most of the time. Every now and then if she did not go, a "ranger boy" went along, or somebody else. Alice did not like to go alone, so she never did.

Buckhorn Ranger Station.   *Helen Dickerson photo, 1930s.*

On a typical mail day Alice drove to the ranger station, about a mile east down the road from the Dickerson home. She picked up the mail from about eighty CCC boys, the ranger and any other neighbor who had brought mail to be collected. Then she drove up

Looking down on Eggers from High Drive.   *Alan Dakan photo, 1930s.*

Eggers Post Office.   *Sanborn photo, 1930s*

and over Pennock Pass and across the High Drive to Eggers in the Poudre Canyon. At the Eggers Post Office she picked up the mail that had been brought up from Bellvue and put it into bags while the Bellvue carrier went on up to Home at the Zimmerman Hotel. Alice then delivered the mailbags to each mailbox on her return trip. The Colorado A&M Pingree Park Forestry Camp mail was left at a big box near the Pennock Pass turnoff from the High

Zimmerman Hotel, Poudre Canyon, 1900.   *Photographer unknown.*

Drive; they had to come down quite a way, at least five miles, from the camp to get the mail. About eighty boys were at the forestry camp, so Alice's little car was always bulging at the seams with mailbags. Other tourist resorts and camps had huge stacks of mail, too. Sam Koenig at Fish Creek, the Lazy D Ranch, Tom Bennett and Frank Koenig on the west side of the pass all had bundles of mail.

"Sometimes that little car was so full of mailbags and packages I could hardly see out," said Helen.

To finish the route, Alice drove up and over the narrow Pennock Pass road again, down to the Hammond place and back to the ranger station where eager CCC boys awaited news from home. She then drove back home, arriving about noon if everything had gone right.

The road at that time could be extremely slippery in spots; it was just a single-track road.

"The road over the pass was like driving on a shelf," Alice said. "You had to be extremely careful how you drove. It was kind of scary sometimes." Ed. note: Scary SOMETIMES! Pennock Pass is practically a single-track road now, in 1994. It stirs up the imagination to picture how it was in those days...and with "vintage" cars.

Bluebirds occasionally selected mailboxes for nesting sites. The girls carefully hung the heavy canvas mailbags on the outsides of boxes so as not to disturb the anxious little blue parents. Likewise, the people who owned the boxes were very careful in removing the bags for the same reason.

"Sometimes they were working on the road where they had a landslide and we didn't get up there 'til late and people wondered what in the world happened to me," Alice recalled. "If I didn't get there with their mail when they thought I should, they were waiting at the mailbox. Sometimes there was high water coming out onto the road and people wondered whether I could make it or not," she said. "Once in awhile the Little South (Poudre) would be out on the road and I kind of worried whether it would be O.K. and whether or not I could get through."

Even the road in front of the Dickerson cabin was just one track wide and it was a higher shelf than in later years. Some of the locations have since been changed.

Occasional delays were unavoidable, but the majority of the time Alice brought the mail through on time.

"One day the mail was detained by a blast in the Poudre

Canyon Narrows. The Bellvue mail carrier had to wait a few hours on the east side of the blast, so we had to wait at Eggers to get the mail," said Helen. Alice added, with a little laugh, "We sneaked off and went up Cameron Pass. Why sit and wait?"

Occasionally the girls stopped to put out fires people left burning on the High Drive. They borrowed shovels and cans of water from the Eggers Post Office and drove back up to extinguish them. That, of course, made them late with the mail and they encountered some impatient people waiting at their mailboxes.

"I took the ranger boy with me one day—Helen didn't want to go. We had a heavy hailstorm, about 6" hail on the other side of the pass," Alice recalled. "I'd stop at the mailboxes and could hardly get my car going again. It was just like trying to go in sand —zzzzzzzzzzzzzzzzzzzzzzzzzzzzzzzzzzzzzzzzzzzzzzzzz— nothing. Finally when we got home the hail had stopped and it hadn't even rained there. It stopped just like a curtain."

The Flower Gatherers

They read at night in black and white
The Wild Flower book so they'd learn;
'Twas plants they dug and hoped no bug
Would ruin the flower or fern.
Colmers were late with the payment date
'Cause they waited for the plants to grow;
The girls worked hard, but their hopes were jarred
So they wrote and told them, "no go!"

Alice and Helen entered into another venture during the 1930s, one that was educational but not too profitable. Somehow the California Wild Flower Nursery in Dos Rios, California, got in touch with the girls asking them to procure plants and seeds for them. The girls bought a book to study so they would know what they were doing. But the book was not in color, so it was even more difficult.

The sisters began the project with great enthusiasm, but swiftly their zeal started to wane. They had to wait until the plants were up and had flowers on them before they could tell what they were. Before shipping them to California they had to ship them to the entomology building at Colorado A & M in Fort Collins. There they were removed from their packaging and examined carefully for any possible disease or insect. Finally they were tagged by the entomologists and shipped to their destination.

Correspondence traveled back and forth from California to Eggers. An example:

Jan. 23, 1936
Miss Helen Dickerson
Masonville Colo.

Dear Miss Dickerson,
 We have not checked over the seeds yet, but, should have them out this month. We have completed a new home and we have had our hands full as it is impossible to hire anyone around here to do any work since the Goverment pays them to do nothing.
 We have had a warm winter so many plants are already comin up. We also had nearly forty inches of rain in three weeks and that was plenty.

The nursery did not pay until they saw whether or not they would grow. Alice said dryly, "That was nice of them; wait 'til next year to pay for them. They wanted the plants so they could sell them. They also wanted little aspen trees—little native plants. We sent them over 300 mariposa lily plants which we got on Fletcher Hill. We finally decided not to mess with them anymore. It was a headache, so we quit."

Gathering wildflowers up on the Cirque, Mummy Range.
Helen Dickerson photo, 1935.

127

The Boys

They had a good time and spent every dime
At Cheyenne Frontier Days——a ball!
A very small group, they went in the coupe;
The turtleback held Helen and Paul.
The cab was a palace for Sheldon and Alice--
Sitting ever so close wasn't bad;
But they didn't arrive 'til next morning at five
At home and was Pop ever mad!

In 1932 a couple of boys from Ohio came in a Model T Ford and thought they would stay all summer. Sam and Allen had met them the previous fall when they visited Ohio. This created a new lease on life for everyone on the homestead, especially the girls. Part of the time they worked, part they played and at times they did absolutely nothing. The boys, Sheldon Sproull and Paul Ramsey, stayed over with Grandpa and Allen. Indeed, they brought a new dimension to the hard-working folks at the Dickerson Ranch.

Having the boys there helped a lot; the Dickerson men took advantage of the extra manpower to help with the haying and

Allen, Sheldon and Paul with hay wagon.   Helen Dickerson photo, 1932.

improve their water system. Originally the family got water from a little spring which was covered by a lidded box. Earl discovered where the cows were getting water up near the barn and thought he could develop a spring there. He, the two boys, Grandpa and

Alice: "Pop had this kind of hay mower."

Allen dug the line and put in the pipe, which Allen had salvaged from a fire in Denver. It took most of the summer to dig the pipeline by hand 5' deep. Only Earl's house was served by the pipeline. Alice and Allen went to Denver to get a lavatory, which Earl installed in the bathroom. The waste water, instead of quietly

Alice: "We had this kind of hay rake."

slipping away through a pipe, drained through a hole near the user's feet. This simplified plumbing procedure was at first rather startling to friends and relatives. After removing the stopper from the sink, water gushed onto the floor and they leaped back in shock. But at least it worked. And they had hot water! "We have wonderful-tasting cold spring water and a hot water tank on the wood stove to heat it," said Alice, and anyone who tasted the water agreed.

One lazy day Sheldon was lying in his car asleep with his feet sticking out the window. Ornery Allen stuck a sign on his feet which read, "Post No Bills". Every time a car came along they saw it, backed up, read it, laughed and drove on up the road.

Sheldon was a real bookworm and read everything he could

get his hands on. One night he was reading and the other three men had gone to bed. While trying to concentrate, little rattling noises kept interrupting his train of thought. Finally he got up, set a mousetrap and before long he had caught six mice. He got tired of re-setting the trap, so he put all six tails in it and just left it there until Sam came down in the morning.

"Grandpa thought it was so funny he came down to our house and told us about it; six mouse tails in the trap and mice hanging out the other end," recalled Alice, chuckling.

In July, all four of the young people went to Cheyenne Frontier Days in Alice's little coupe. They fastened the "turtleback" (trunk) up with a rope so the lid would not fall down on Helen's and Paul's heads and away they went, with Sheldon and Alice in the cab. They had an absolutely wonderful day. On the way home they got caught in a cloudburst.

"We weren't about to go up the Buckhorn that night because sometimes the road went out," Alice said, defensively. "We couldn't see the road and there was terrific lightning. We just parked down by Masonville. Just sat and talked." Laugh, laugh.

"We got home next morning at 5:00 a.m. and Pop was mad. He'd liked to have killed the boys and disowned us. He hadn't cared if we went to Cheyenne, but he didn't think it was very nice we stayed all night. But he didn't do anything; just pouted. It's a wonder he didn't tell the boys to get out. He didn't want any boys around. He was afraid he'd lose us, I guess; we were his hired hands," said Alice. "I don't know if it was because he wanted us here to work or whether he just didn't want us to get married. I could have married several times, but I didn't. It was the same with Helen. Her Ohio boyfriend was Paul Ramsey. She was very fond of him, but if she was disappointed he married someone else, she never let on. We corresponded with Paul and his wife for years until he died."

One night three boys came and serenaded the girls. Pop blew his cool that time, too, and told them to get out.

*Helen Dickerson and
Paul Ramsey.
Photo by Alice, 1932.*

Earl did not want his daughters to go with anybody. One time Alice and Helen met two boys at the feed store in Fort Collins. The young men invited the girls to go with them to a lecture on bulls at the National Western Stock Show in Denver, followed by a red-carpet banquet. The girls got all dressed up and drove to Fort Collins, where they met the boys. The fellows had been there the previous year and recalled they had enjoyed a nice banquet. But this time they gave them "a little piece of cake and a dab of ice cream," said Alice, disgusted. "So we went out to supper and a picture show and again didn't get home 'til 5:00 a.m." On the way home up the Buckhorn, Helen said to her sister, "You're driving

131

Alice Dickerson and Sheldon Sproull. Photo by Helen, 1932.

a little bit strange, aren't you?" To which Alice replied, "Well, I guess I'm getting sleepy." And Pop was furious again.

Sam

Grandpa was born on a warm summer morn;
The Fourth of July was the day.
They all came with food in a fine picnic mood;
"Everyone honors my day," he'd say.
Sam claimed his stake in Colorado state
And proved he was up to the chore;
A smithy by trade, fine work he made
And his son picked up on the lore.

Through the years Grandpa Sam kicked his alcohol habit, which was what the family had hoped when they moved to the mountains. He had also been a part of making the homestead work. The family certainly did not get rich, but they toughed it out, worked hard and became accustomed to the rural mountain way of life.

Alice always liked Grandpa, but was not with him much. He was always just there. In the spring and summer Sam always picked bouquets of flowers for Stella.

One time Sam wanted to take the team and wagon to meet Allen and Earl coming up the Poudre in Allen's car because the Buckhorn road had washed out. He and Alice hitched up the team, packed a lunch and away they went. After crossing the pass, they unhitched the horses and made a fire, like old times. They were enjoying it so much they accidentally caught the grass on fire and almost did not get it out. Finally Allen and Earl came along and helped them snuff the fire. Alice and Grandpa took Allen and Earl home because deep mudholes prevented Allen's car from going any farther that day.

They celebrated his 84th birthday on July 4, 1937. Sam always said, "Everybody celebrates my birthday."

The 4th of July always was a big day at the homestead as long as Sam was alive. "Several of the relatives would come from Eaton, Greeley and Windsor in buggies and stay a few days," recalled Helen. "Several of the neighbors around here would come. All brought special food and generally we went to the gulch back of Grandpa's house and spread blankets under the big spruce trees to picnic on. Quite often there were twenty or more of us. We

133

didn't build campfires for those occasions; I guess we had enough campfires while clearing the land. Some of the folks would get a little fishing done while they were here. Grandpa's last birthday cake looked like a porcupine, it had so many candles on it."

"Yes, and by the time the last candle was being lit, the first one was already burned down to the frosting," added Alice.

Sam Doney Dickerson 1853-1937. Helen Dickerson photo, 1930s.

Not long after that when Alice and Helen were on the mail route one day, Alice exclaimed, "My goodness, there's Grandpa over there." He had gone to meet them and had walked over to the High Drive through Monument Gulch, a distance of about six miles, and was standing by the the mailbox near the Little South. "He should not have been doing that," said Alice, still distressed about it. "If we had not seen him when we did, we would never have known where he was. It was only a short time after that that he died."

Sam became ill and one of his sons took him to a hospital in Denver. While he was ill, Allen took the "crank" telephone down for Earl's family to use. It was a wonderful addition to their home. Sam passed away in August, 1937, and was buried in Windsor, next to his wife. Five members of the Dickerson family remained on the ranch.

IV
BUSY LITTLE VALLEY
1937-1942

Ranch in Full Swing

Times were so bad, but the family was glad
  For the garden, milk, eggs and meat;
They almost shed tears when they sold three big steers
  At eleven mere dollars apiece.
They felled a big pine and were shocked to find
  Three tiny squirrels unmarred;
A house they built soon, fed the babes with a spoon,
  And they lived several years in the yard.

Summer at the Dickersons' in the late 30s and early 40s found the place teeming with activity. The sawmill was running, Helen was selling souvenirs at her little stand, the garden was flourishing, cows were grazing and Stella was not only feeding the family, but usually boarders, too.

Always Earl had tried to be a cattleman after he moved to the mountains. He had a herd of about 40 cows, all milk cow types and just scrubs. During the depression Earl sold the cattle that were not good milk cows. He may as well have butchered them all himself for what he got out of them. Three 1100 pound steers brought him eleven dollars each...and the Dickersons had to help herd them to Windsor. It was a bad time when they did not make much money. T-bone steaks were only about forty cents a pound and eggs eleven cents a dozen. Allen and Earl kept the sawmill running through the years. Helen continued to milk the cows and Alice fed them. Alice separated the milk, hauled the cream to town and helped make cheese and other products to sell.

Allen was always a timber man. He did not work at anything else, not even cattle. Sometimes he had to be gone, so Earl once in awhile would enlist Alice to help cut logs. They cut down the trees and then used seven or 8-foot long crosscut saws to saw it into log lengths. "Those saws were all we had; just hand saws," recalled Alice a little bitterly. "We couldn't cut the whole forest down that way, though, like they do with chain saws. I cut seven hundred feet one day. I said 'that's enough'. I don't want to cut logs."

Allen and Earl moved the sawmill down the Buckhorn about three miles for convenience because they were getting their timber from the Forest Service up on the mountain. They left their big Case tractor with which they cut the logs, the lumber and other equipment down there while they went home at night. Someone stole lumber from their site, but, though they had an idea who the thieves were, they never did catch them.

Sawmill three miles down the Buckhorn.   Photo Helen Dickerson, 1930s.

One day the men cut down a tree with axes and a hand-powered crosscut saw and, to their surprise, found a nest of three tiny hairless closed-eyed baby Abert squirrels. Earl placed them in a big pail, nest and all. Helen and Alice built a little house and fed them with teaspoons until they were old enough to fend for themselves. The squirrels, two grey and one black, lived in their yard for several years.

Abert Squirrels.
Photo by Alice Dickerson.

When Allen was doing some road work for Ranger Smith on Pennock Pass, he set a dynamite charge and yelled, "Fire!" Soon the blast went off sending rocks flying down into the gulch where Roy Hyatt had temporarily stored a pile of mine props. Suddenly an unidentified truck drove away in a big hurry. Noticing the load of props on the truck, Allen thought quickly, wrote down the license number and reported him to Smith. The culprit was apprehended and Smith made him bring back the stolen props and unload them at Hyatt's place in Masonville. Dickersons thought he should have to take them back to where he stole them, but it was better for Hyatt the way Smith did it; he received free delivery of his props!

Ralph Derby staggered down off the pass one day and told Allen he went off the road. When they got up there, Derby said, "Isn't too bad, is it, Allen?" Allen cringed. The car was at an incredible angle over the bank on the top of the pass and Ralph was drunk, as always. Allen got the car out, but it was a hard and dangerous job. Butch Hersh always said if you shake hands with Ralph, shake both hands; he may have the other one in your pocket.

They were not at the ranch every minute; Earl and his daughters were always interested in another source of income and satisfaction of curious minds. Earl, Helen and Alice traveled over the pass one beautiful summer day to join Sam Steele in hunting crystals up on a mountain behind his cabin. The mission was a success; they brought home about one hundred pounds of crystals of all colors and sizes.

One visitor to the Dickerson homestead around 1940 was Frank Kalen, a year-long Crystal Mountain resident. An excellent lapidarist, he could cut silica to look like diamonds. Among his finds were gem garnets and aquamarine-variety beryl, pure emeralds, as clear as green water. At Alice's request, he made a beautiful Redfeather amethyst ring for her. However, he was later found to be one of Hitler's spies and moved, not of his own choosing, to Fort Leavenworth Prison.

Alice and Allen left to go fishing at Twin Lakes in Allen's Model T truck one day. While climbing up over Pennock Pass, Alice looked down off the sharpest curve, saw a truck coming and then saw it go off the edge. They drove back down and found the Pickets, who had drunk a little too much beer. Allen pulled them out and they all spent the rest of the day fishing and eating a picnic dinner.

If Alice was in the wrong place at the right time in her little coupe, she could get behind Andy and Henry Morrison's herd of sheep. The brothers pastured sheep many years on Signal Mountain and, to get them there, drove them on the Buckhorn Road, past Sherwoods' and over the mountains. It was the Buckhorn road in its narrow little canyon that could delay a car for quite a long time if it tried to get through the huge herd of sheep traveling in the same direction.

For two years before World War II the young folks from the Buckhorn, Pingree Park and Poudre Canyon got together almost every other week throughout the summer. They varied the location, activities ranging from cookouts at campgrounds, box suppers at the Eggers School, square dances at Eggers or a dance and supper the last night of summer school at the Pingree Park Forestry School. The parties were never started again when the war was over; the young folks had scattered to the winds and some had been lost in the war, especially one boy the Dickerson family liked so much. He was killed within the first five hours on Iwo Jima.

CCC Boys

They came in mobs, the boys with jobs—
Their group was the CCCs;
Built roads and trails, these fine young males
And fought fires to save the trees.
Their dynamite blast made the ranger mad fast—
Fruit jars fell off and broke;
But when he turned around not a boy was found;
They'd vanished like wisps of smoke.

CCC Boys.
Photo by Helen Dickerson, 1930s.

Seven Civilian Conservation Corps (CCC) boys from Oklahoma boarded with the Dickersons and stayed at their cabin. They "cruised the timber" which, in non-logger talk, means estimating how much timber is in an area in so many thousands of square feet. This was done on the Ballard Unit the winter before Bockman bought the timber.

The CCC was a federal program in which thousands of unemployed young men found instructive work under the direction of U.S. Army officers and other experienced men in the art of

CCC Boys cruising the timber.
Helen Dickerson Photo, 1930s.

leadership. The program was perfectly adapted to Colorado with its vast forest reserves. Enrolled for six months in groups of one hundred and seventy-five members, the workers built roads and trails, fought forest fires and engaged in many other worth-while projects. The high country under the domain of the Mummy Range was no exception.

One of the rangers who had been stationed at the Buckhorn Ranger Station from 1913 to 1918, Kenson Helmick, returned after he left the Forest Service to become foreman at the CCC camp located where the present Fish Creek Campground is and on both sides of the road. The camp contained 200 boys.

Old White Pine Fire Tower. Pre-1937.
Forest Service photo.

CCC boys built the White Pine fire tower, completed in 1939. Their camp was located near the Ranger Station. Lumber was carried by hand to the site and window glass was transported by a narrow horse-drawn cart. Later a CCC Camp where the original log ranger station was (across from where the present ranger station is) had facilities for eighty boys, including tent cabins and a big mess hall.

While the CCC boys were at their camp down by the ranger station, many often became homesick. At least that was their excuse when they walked up to the Dickersons on the nice summer evenings. They and the family played games and Earl usually entertained them with the radio until he tired of it and went to bed. Alice and Helen did a lot of photography for the boys who also

141

Original Buckhorn Ranger Station.　　　　*Photo by Alan Dakan, 1930s.*

enjoyed watching Helen develop their pictures. Stella and the girls always had some home-baked snacks for them. Being at the cozy cabin with the gracious Dickersons certainly beat leisure time life at the barracks. However, it was probably a good thing all the boys did not come at once to the tiny Dickerson cabin.

Some of the CCC boys installed the septic system for the new ranger station. But one day they set such a heavy charge of dynamite that the blast shook the glass fruit jars off the shelves in Ranger Smith's basement. Some of the jars that the Dickerson ladies had helped Mrs. Smith can broke into pieces and made a splendid mess. Ranger Smith was so mad he told them if they wanted to blow the place up, just wait a bit and he and his wife would move out.

The present ranger station was built by Guy and Harold Fowler. Harold and his family lived in the Dickerson cabin and he ran from the cabin one mile to the ranger station morning, noon and night. The CCC boys moved the Forest Service office over to its present location. Earl Dickerson hauled the dirt from Monument Gulch with team and wagon for the ranger's house yard.

When the WPA widened the road through Deadman Canyon and Fletcher Hill, Earl and Allen worked for the foreman, Floyd Mason, one winter. They stayed in Masonville during the week

New Ranger Station. Photo by Alan Dakan, 1930s.

and went home weekends. No machinery of any kind was used on that project, which was to create work for the unemployed; only picks and shovels were used.

The boys removed the telephone poles from the old Estes Park Trail, which not only ended that telephone line, but placed both the trail and line into the annals of history.

Old Ranger Station and barn.   *Photo by Alan Dakan.*

' 39 Pickup, 39 Years

"Call the Dickerson bunch if you want a good lunch"
Was the cry of men working hard;
"They'll welcome you there with a smile and a chair
From their door you are never barred."
The coupe went to town and a pickup was found
'Twas a lemon and brought Alice to tears;
A '39 truck next, but it sure wasn't hexed—
She drove it for 39 years!

During the summer of 1938 there were ten lightning fires in one week. Assistant Ranger Walter Hanson came back from a hard day's fighting to the Dickersons' where he was rooming and boarding and ate supper at 9:00 p.m. He was exhausted and went to bed immediately after supper. At 1:00 a.m. Ranger Frank Smith called and asked the Dickersons to get Walter up, feed him breakfast and pack him a lunch; a fire was raging on Crystal Mountain. Poor Walter thought that was the most tasteless breakfast he ever ate in his sleepy exhausted stupor. He was gone firefighting for a few days. The three Dickerson ladies decided to prepare stewed tomatoes, his favorite, for him when he returned. To the dismay of everyone, most of all Walter, stewed tomatoes were almost all he had eaten while fighting the fire. A great variety of food had been available, but not where he was working. He was sick of stewed tomatoes. Helen said, "This may sound like Walter was hard to cook for, but he wasn't."

Haying time: a friend, Earl and Sam, 1930s. Helen Dickerson photo.

Earl, Helen and Alice did the haying in the meadow below the ranger station. Even after Earl died in later years, the girls still did the haying. Helen plowed part of the field a few years with a riding plow pulled by a team of horses; then planted oats. Earl cut it and Helen raked there for many years. They had established a regular routine: Alice stomped down the hay on the wagon, Earl cut and pitched it and Helen drove the horses. They took it up to their place and stored it in three big hay sheds. Alice and Helen also helped stack hay one fall when Albert Chandler lived on the Little Beaver, where Mr. Rockwell had a haystacker.

Every year the garden was improved. After using a walking plow for many years with Helen driving the team, they started digging with a shovel. This method enabled them to dig close to the edges and prevented the horses from tromping out the perennials while turning around ends of the garden.

Experimentation went on year after year trying to find plant varieties which would grow and produce successfully in the short high altitude growing season. Stella experimented often with growing tomatoes and finally, by covering them every night, she succeeded in ripening two or three. One year she had enough green tomatoes to make several quarts of green tomato mincemeat. They tried corn, but the cobs froze off. Then sunflowers, but they froze before they even had a flower on them, although Alice did get one sunflower to bloom one year before it was zapped by the frost. Once in awhile summer squash and string beans made it. The girls' cousin, Albert Foster, helped develop a cross between wild and tame strawberries, called "Radiance". It worked well in Albert's harsh Wyoming growing conditions, but after working well for a few years on the Buckhorn, the plants reverted back to little wild ones. Their aspen ground proved to be excellent for lettuce. They sold bushels of it to some Windsor stores. They also produced bushels of sweet mountain peas and dried them for winter use. Sometimes they took bushels of peas down to Munn's Gardens in Fort Collins and traded for fruit and vegetables they could not raise. Helen brought home whole stalks of bananas, eleven pounds to a crate, and sold them at her stand for twenty cents a pound. Cucumbers, melons and peanuts did not even make a good start. But carrots, turnips, rutabagas, head lettuce, cabbage, broccoli, parsnips, beets, chard, spinach, dill and mustard all grew well most years. As Alice explained, "Our garden didn't have much of a growing season, but what we did raise was extra good. Better than you'd get anyplace else. Some rutabagas and turnips weighed over 5 pounds each."

Alice traded her little coupe for a 1936 pickup, which she

drove for about a year. But it did not suit Alice. "I called it a lemon," she said. "I might as well paint a lemon on the thing," and with that she went back to town and bought a 1939 Chevrolet pickup. She needed a non-lemon type vehicle she could absolutely rely on to carry her up and over the pass, back and forth on the High Drive and into the Poudre Canyon. She needed more room for the piles of mail and packages. The mail must go through. And it did. She was to drive that old reliable pickup for 39 years!

The Hunters

Life was not dull,
*   there was hardly a lull*
At the Dickerson place
*   in the hills;*
Earl fired the machine
*   to get up some steam—*
Loud toots shook
*   the window sills;*
The hunter should have heard
*   'cause it scared every bird*
And they heard it
*   near Estes Park!*
He wandered in beat
*   with cold aching feet*
Glad it was no longer dark.

One never knew when a day's plans would be foiled by unexpected events. One day someone spotted the sky full of smoke on top of Pennock Pass, so Alice, Helen and Allen threw tools in Alice's pickup and drove up to the fire, leaving Stella trying to get Ranger Smith and anyone else she could think of to help. Allen and the girls almost had a ditch completed around the hot-burning fire before anyone else got there. Ranger Smith and Tom and Joe Bennett arrived about the same time and Tom thought they ought to call in some CCC boys. But Smith, digging furiously with the Dickersons, said, "We have good help now; we don't need any." Alice and Helen drove up and down the pass hauling water in barrels from their spring to spray with hand pumps. Earl managed to milk the cows; he was too crippled to fight fires or milk much, but he did it, which freed the girls to work on the fire until 9:00 or 10:00 p.m. Allen and Smith stayed on most of the night as a big wind came up to keep the fire fanned. Earl had been fire warden until he became too crippled to do much; then Allen accepted the job.

No elk were ever seen in the eastern shadows of the Mummy until the late 1930s. They were first spotted on Crystal Mountain, then Sherwoods' and Ballards'. The first elk season was established in 1937 and it started off with a bang.

Allen was rudely awakened one night by several highpowered

rifle shots right in front of his cabin. He vaulted furiously outside and yelled, in different words than are written here, "What do you think you are doing?" Hastily apologizing, the men told Allen one of their hunting party was missing, so they thought he might hear shots and come toward the direction from which they were fired. They explained that the last they had seen of him, he was tracking an elk south off Pennock Pass. The shots had brought no results, so the next morning Earl started a fire in the boiler to get steam for the whistle. Then they began a series of three very loud blasts, waiting quite awhile between each group of three, hoping the lost hunter would follow the sound. This was continued until noon, when a bedraggled man came dragging up the road carrying overshoes and rifle. By that time search parties were wandering all over the mountains looking for him. They asked the exhausted hunter if he was lost, and he guessed he was. Gratefully, he hobbled into the warmth of the Dickerson cabin, where he ate heartily of Stella's culinary offerings, then got sick in the middle of the busy kitchen.

After the cleanup the naive hunter told the listening ears around the kitchen table that he did not pay any attention to the loud steam whistle because he did not know what it had meant. He said he had used up his matches trying to get his handkerchief and comb to burn and admitted the only food he had with him was a candy bar. He had finally inadvertently come across to the Crystal Mountain road and followed it to the Buckhorn. Fortunately for the searchers, he came up to the Dickersons' instead of wandering off down the Buckhorn. Meanwhile, the hapless hunter rejuvenated himself and Earl tooted the whistle more frequently in an effort to call in the searchers. Eventually they all arrived and thankfully left for home. But not before they all had a good laugh when the sheriff, Carol Gooch, told them he had heard the whistle loud and clear over at Miller's Fork near Estes Park. The Dickersons received a nice thank-you note from the lost hunter, who worked for a Fort Collins newspaper.

A year or two after the lost hunter incident, another hunter staying with his hunting party in the Bosworth cabin on Stove Prairie ventured out in a dense fog to hunt deer and failed to return to camp. A day or so later his wife and other family members stopped to ask Dickersons if they had seen anything of him. Allen gathered all the men he could find and the search party began scouring the country while the wife and son stayed in the Dickerson home crying. Allen led the searchers to a high cliff of rocks on the Rockwell place that he thought could be in line with the Bosworth cabin, but found no one. When the searchers returned that night with no good news, the poor woman cried while looking out the window, "My poor, poor husband!"

The family returned to Longmont and the search continued for weeks. Allen, Ranger Frank Smith, the sheriff and a group of CCC boys combed the Stove Prairie district. The men tried to get the boys to fan out, but every time they peeked around at them, the timid boys were in close single file again. Later, airplanes dipped in and out of valleys, but to no avail.

Two years later a poaching trapper found the man's skeleton when he reached behind a big log to get leaves to cover his illegal traps. He also found his rifle on the cliff of rocks where Allen had led the searchers the first day they started the search. The trapper was fined, but his reward for finding the man was greater than his fine.

The elevation printed on the sign on top of Pennock Pass (9143') was taken from an altimeter Sam Dickerson had retrieved from an Eaton street in the 1800s after a buggy had run over it and cracked its face. "Fools' names and fools' faces always appear in public places" is a time-worn saying. A fool once carved his name and address on the Pennock sign, making it simple for Ranger Smith to collect the fine, which he did.

One fine summer day sometime in 1942 the girls were working in the garden when they saw a very old, stooped man coming slowly up the road. When he was near enough so they could hear him, he asked where the soddy was. Curious, the girls showed him where it had been on the bank; the road had changed, so he did not recognize where it had been. They were pleased when he told them he was Mr. Lytle. Alice said, "That mountain to the west is named for you." The old man left, looking pleased and satisfied.

High Country Winter

Weird things were done 'neath the cold winter sun
When the snows piled heavy and deep;
The road ruts they'd ride they'd best abide
Or they'd end up cold in the creek;
Snow was the most when it covered the posts--
Cows hung on the fence so loose.
Earl heard a honk as they rode along;
My word! 'Twas a Christmas goose!

Dickerson country was not too conducive to keeping livestock through the winter. Taking care of the livestock proved to be a difficult chore in deep snow.

Helen Dickerson in one of the heavier snows.
Photo by Stella, 4-22-32.

A path had to be shoveled to trail the horses and cattle to water. Sometimes over-eager animals would not wait for that and bounded out and around the shovelers and ended up having to be shoveled out themselves. Sometimes the fence and corral posts were completely buried. Once an oblivious cow wandered across the pole fence surrounding the corral, high-centered herself and became entangled in the poles. Earl was furious. In defense of the cow, the fence was so obscured she could not see it and the packed snow had held her up until her front feet had crossed over the fence; then she sank so her feet were on both sides. In defense of Earl, his knee hurt, he was tired and cold and he had to knock down the poles to get the obstinate critter out.

One day a horse came running down the trail towards the house instead of the other direction toward the water, and Stella tried to head it off. The animal got to floundering and became tangled in the wagon under the snow. It became so wild and panicky that Stella had to plunge into the deep snow to avoid getting injured by flailing hoofs. The horse soon got itself up, ran to the end of the trail, then back to where it belonged.

Deep snows of that kind had to be shoveled off roofs, as they began to sag.

After visiting relatives in Greeley and Windsor before Christmas one year, Helen met Earl and Allen in Masonville. They loaded her and all her gear, including a live goose she had bought for Christmas dinner and spent the night at Chandlers. The next day they loaded up for the journey home. When they arrived at Deadman Canyon, they were startled by a honk, so pulled to the edge of the road. Then, feeling sheepish, they pulled back onto the road realizing that what they heard had come from that goose.

Earl and Allen got stuck in a big snowdrift coming down Sherwood Hill in the Model T one very cool evening. They walked home, each carrying a gunny sack of groceries on his back. When they arrived home, Earl told his family he sensed something or someone was following them on the way home in the dark. The next morning they went down with the team and wagon to retrieve the car and found large cougar tracks in their footprints all the way from the car to the ranger station.

Stella was ill in the hospital for quite some time in the winter of 1941-42. She had hit her head on a 2x4 in the chicken house,

Cougar tracks.

causing a slight cerebral hemorrhage. In time she recovered and showed no sign of it ever again, except she appeared to have aged ten years.

They still had cows and chickens and, during a cold spell, were almost out of grain. Alice and Helen started for town, but had many stops shoveling snowdrifts. They arrived at Masonville in six hours, then drove to Fort Collins to get the grain. They had left Earl at home not feeling well, so the girls intended to get home that night. But people at the Masonville Post Office stopped them and told them that Allen had called; they were not to attempt getting home. He and Brad Ramsey had gone to town to register for the World War II draft and they had been forced to walk home on shortcuts over the mountains. Helen said, "We were so tired we wouldn't have made it anyway." Next morning Allen and Brad met the girls near the ranger station and helped shovel and push their way home.

When the girls brought their mother home the next spring, the road was just two deep ruts.

"If you left the ruts, you would be in the creek. We got stuck in a mud hole and spent hours getting out. One wouldn't think it would be so hard to find rocks in the Rocky Mountains.... even in the dark," Helen said.

Allen read the measurements on a snow board down the hill from the Dickerson home for several years. Eleven feet was the average annual snowfall.

Piled higher and deeper.   *Helen Dickerson photo, 1930s.*

Ohio

She wanted to roam and leave her home--
How she envied the free-flying crow;
Uncle Allen knew this, so he couldn't miss;
To Ohio he asked her to go.
On a Greyhound bus without a fuss
Alice joyfully climbed inside;
Dickerson kin she met with a grin
When she left, Winona cried.

Allen and Alice Dickerson, 5-20-41. Ohio.
Photo by Winona Dickerson.

Alice had never been farther from home than Denver, Greeley and Cheyenne. She was disenchanted with her father because even after she was in her 30s, he still dominated her life. Consequently, she did not want to stay home any more than necessary.

Allen had previously traveled to Ohio with his father to visit relatives when Alice had been in Windsor. This time he wanted her to accompany him on a repeat trip. Happily, at age 32, she climbed onto a Greyhound bus with her uncle Allen Dickerson and off they went to Roscoe, Ohio after Easter, 1941.

Winona and Alice. Photo by
Allen Dickerson, 1941.

Alice had a wonderful time and became very fond of a delightful cousin, Winona Dickerson, whom she had never met. The two young ladies spent more than a month together touring, hiking and just enjoying each other's company. Allen got lost once, and the two ladies almost called the sheriff, but thought better of it. Allen found his way back all by himself.

Alice was not the least bit upset when a Greyhound bus strike stopped them from returning to Colorado on schedule; it gave Alice and Winona more time together.

Meanwhile, back at the ranch, June first had rolled around and Helen pinch-hit for Alice on the mail route; she had never driven a car, so she had to get someone to drive for her.

Alice and Winona corresponded often for the next fifty one years, but never saw each other again. Winona passed away late in 1992.

Winona Dickerson's house, Roscoe , Ohio, 1941.
Photo by Allen Dickerson.

Pop Passes On

Earl had known strife, but had a good life
  Carving a home in the woods;
He injured his knee, which painful would be;
  It affected his production of goods.
Two daughters had he, as fine as could be--
  He loved them and taught them his tricks;
He had a stout heart, but it failed and wouldn't start,
  So he left the family in a fix.

The United States Forest Service in 1942 awarded a contract to Earl to cut 40,000' of bridge plank, with the Forest Service bringing the logs to the mill. But Earl Dickerson was ill, having had a heart attack. On September 4, 1942, Alice was driving her father to the doctor in Fort Collins when a fellow on the wrong side of the road hit her pickup. Her father died in her arms of another heart attack right there on the spot. Damage to her pickup was so extensive it had to be repaired before she could drive home. The awful incident also destroyed her love for driving; after that she drove only when absolutely necessary.

Both Alice and Helen were proud that all the Forest Service rangers, their supervisors and some Colorado State University professors attended their father's funeral. The rangers served as pall bearers; Earl Dickerson was buried in Fort Collins.

Earl Ross Dickerson 1879-1942.
Photo by Helen Dickerson 1940.

V.
DETERMINATION
AND GRIT
1942-1964

Allen's bath house.

Life Gets Really Tough

They worked at the mill, Pop's contract to fill,
And Helen milked the cows down;
Still carried the mail, poured cream in a pail
And took it to sell in town.
Alice loathed the mill, said women it'd kill
So she quit and shouted with glee;
The mail route closed, due to war, they supposed;
Sadness, 'cause she had liked being free.

Alice and Helen had never worked at the sawmill when their father was living. They had helped haul logs when they had to, but that was the extent of it. But the big contract their father had been awarded hung in limbo; Allen needed help if the terms of the contract were to be met. So Helen and a neighbor pitched in and worked hard with Allen to honor the Forest Service contract. Alice joined the crew later. It was very difficult for the girls; not only was it all new to them, but they could not get men to work because World War II was in progress. Ironically, the girls had difficulty getting gloves, because gloves were rationed to working men. Helen and Alice were only about five feet in height and, though always in excellent condition, nevertheless were diminutive for such heavy work. Through determination and hard work, they did complete the plank order in the allotted time. But it took

Allen, Helen and Alice at the sawmill, 9-25-45.
Fred Johnson, USFS photographer.

its toll; Alice injured her arm when Helen inadvertently dropped her end of a heavy plank, and it never did heal.

Having gotten into the swing of things, the girls worked at the sawmill for ten years after completing the plank contract. Besides run-of-the-mill lumber orders, they and Allen sawed thousands of feet of lodgepole pine into saddle timber for a Denver saddle manufacturing company during World War II; the U.S. Army needed saddles. The Dickersons provided 2x8s for the cantles, 2x6s for the seats and 4x4s for the pommels. As was always a characteristic of the Dickerson girls, they were not satisfied to just provide the lumber; their innate curiosity prompted them, especially Alice, to find out how the saddlemakers used the lumber, so they went to Denver to watch the process.

Alice and Helen, 9-25-45. Fred Johnson, USFS photographer.

During the time Alice was carrying the mail and also working at the sawmill, Allen began making lodgepole pine shingles and the girls helped him. Helen was the "fireman" and Alice did the bundling. He had a little engine he used with which to make the shingles. Originally it had been a steam boiler in a Denver laundry. Allen had bought it and it scared Alice to death bringing it home in her pickup. If he had not gone with her, no way would she have brought it home.

"I could hardly hold the front end on the road; it just danced back and forth...I was scared. Front end kept floating in the air...I know it left the ground. I said I wouldn't haul that thing again for anything. It must have weighed a ton," recalled Alice as goose bumps raised on her arms just reminiscing about the experience.

But they had succeeded in transporting it there. It was what they called their "shingle sawmill" and was comparatively small. The steam came through a pipe from the big engine to the little engine which ran the shingle mill. The Dickersons felt their lodgepole pine shingles were better than others and roofed their own buildings with them.

Another story of Alice's hauling experiences with her now-famous 1939 Chevrolet pickup which she had for 39 years also brought nervous twitches as Alice told it: "I hauled some planks over to the Poudre like that so-called 'little' engine and I said no more of that, either. I thought the thing was going to fly over the cliff. Where you come down to the main Poudre road from the High Drive near the big green house where Trimbles lived before you cross the bridge. I was scared...front end kept floating in the air. It was when I was carrying the mail and I took them over when I was going to the Eggers Post Office."

Allen and the girls sawed three-sided logs for Elizabeth Geiger, who homesteaded in Deadman Canyon before the road was there. Alice and Helen peeled the remaining sides of all the logs for Elizabeth's new log house. Alice dropped one of the heavy logs on her leg and it never did get well. Because no road existed in Deadman Canyon, Elizabeth had to travel over Deadman Hill and down into the canyon to get to her place. A Denver high school woodcrafts teacher, she had built her first house herself out of slabs and made most of her own furniture. Using her place for recreation and horse pasture, she and friends often rode horseback past the Dickerson Ranch on their way to the Mummy Range to study alpine flowers. Often they came back with glowing reports of flowers, Rocky Mountain Bighorn Sheep and other news of life on the alpine tundra. One time Elizabeth came by and told the girls the chokecherry bushes at her cabin looked like a tornado had hit them. A bear and her cubs had invaded her patio and feasted on chokecherries and apple butter she had made and left outdoors. Elizabeth, when finding the bears, screamed at them "Get out of here!" In their panic to get away, they knocked over the apple butter and ran.

Butch Hersh wanted his boys, Elmer, John, Henry and Harry, to get away from downtown influences, so he thought it would be good for them to be up at the Dickersons' with Allen to help with the sawmill, timber and hay. When they were helping, Alice and Helen did not, and it was a relief. The boys stayed until school started. They lived with Allen and cooked their own breakfasts.

One of the Hersh Boys with Allen's log-hauling team. Photo by Helen Dickerson, 1930s.

But the aroma drifting over from the other side of the meadow was too much for them, so they ate most of their lunch and evening meals with Stella and the girls.

A drop in lumber prices forced the family to abandon the sawmill operation. Allen maintained a desultory production sufficient enough to allow him to batch comfortably in his cabin.

Henry Hersh transporting logs to the sawmill. Photo by Helen Dickerson, 1930s.

Alice hated the sawmill work and tired of working there. She quit and never worked there again, saying, "It's hard work hassling those big logs. That isn't women's work. Allen can take care of it himself."

The present Buckhorn road was built in 1964. The big rock ledge exploded with such powerful blasts that the windows and dishes in the little Dickerson cabin rattled.

"Some people called it Little Guadalcanal," laughed Helen. "It doesn't look so bad now after the scars have healed."

Alice remembering logging. Old log barn at Grandpa's.
Photographer unknown, 1952.

Now that Alice had her pickup, she had more room for the piles of mail and packages when she was running the mail route. She carried the mail in front and packages in back and hoped it would not rain, although she always took along a big, heavy canvas with which to cover the payload if necessary...and sometimes it was. They could snap the canvas mailbags shut so the mail inside would not get wet if residents did not get to their mailboxes quickly. Helen usually put the mail in the boxes so Alice did not have to get out of the driver's seat. She hung the bags on a post or whatever they had and picked up bags of mail to send out. Alice did not get to finish her contract, due to the government closing the route because of World War II. She could not carry the mail from "no post office to no post office". But she had carried the mail for almost ten years over narrow precipitous high mountain roads in early unsophisticated vehicles and, except for occasional delays not of her doing, never missed a mail delivery.

Eggers Post Office and '39 Chevy pickup. Photo by Helen Dickerson, 1940.

During World War II Alice and Helen were offered jobs teaching crafts to the disabled war veterans, but at that time they were working at the sawmill and milking cows and it would have meant leaving Stella alone, so they refused.

Helen milked 13 cows for awhile. Alice still fed the cows and separated the milk and once a week Alice and Stella went to Fort Collins to sell cream. Helen did not go very often because she had the stand to look after and all the milking. Plus they both had the sawmill, cooking, sewing, crafts, haying, whacking weeds....

Alice: "I used one of these for a weed whacker. Used it without the cradle."

Alice, if she could find the time, did only what she wanted.

Sometimes after working at the sawmill all day, hiking two miles to get the cows and milking them all—just about to chop wood and help get supper, someone would honk at the stand for Helen. She would run down; all they wanted was information and they would ask, "What in the world do you do with all your time 'way up here?"

Alice at Golden Eagle, 1954.   *Photo by Red Fenwick, **Denver Post**.*

The Innovator

Sugar mixed with water, she sure thought it oughter
Bring a hummer in to sip real quick;
She put it in a vial by a columbine as trial
And played upon the hummingbird a trick.
Soon hummers were stirring, buzzing and a-whirring--
Ninety pounds of sugar vanished fast.
Alice fast could see what joy feeding them could be;
She had started a practice that would last.

Alice Dickerson, reportedly, was the first person to feed hummingbirds. One day she decided to experiment to see if the tiny little birds would come to what she had to offer. She had a little heart-shaped vial fixed on a pin used for attaching a flower to a lapel. She put a little drop of sugar water into the vial which she had painted with red fingernail polish and put it on a stick near a columbine. Almost instantly a hummingbird zoomed in to test the "nectar".

Hummingbird on a barbed wire fence.   *Photo by Miriam Mohr, 1991.*

Greatly encouraged, she and Helen fixed up some little bottles, hung them up all over the place and delighted in watching them come to feed. Before that, they seldom saw a hummingbird. They heard them and occasionally saw one, an event so unusual that one of them would say, "There goes a hummingbird!"

People in Estes Park and on the Poudre did not know about feeding hummingbirds before Alice started feeding them. Before she knew it, she was feeding 90 pounds of sugar during a season. The place was alive with hummingbirds. She was not banding birds then, but she had been feeding birds and squirrels for a number of years.

Alive with hummingbirds.   *Photo by Alice Dickerson.*

Resort Laborers
and
Pine Cone Gatherers

Dolly needed aid, so plans the ladies made
  To drive to Glen Echo and toil.
They washed clothes, made beds, kept orders in their heads,
  Cleaned cabins, pumped gas and changed the oil.
Ate when they could, cleaned the kitchen, stacked the wood
  And Stella cooked for guests three times a day.
Sixteen hours each of seven days a week;
  She worked them to death for little pay.

The three Dickerson ladies continued to work as hard or harder than any man did, whether it was hauling milk and cream, dragging, chopping and sawing wood, handling logs or putting up hay, in addition to the everyday household chores. Helen was beginning to think the thirteen cows were goats, not cows, due to the meager amounts of milk they gave. But what extra milk they did have, it was used to fatten calves for market. They continued to cook for male boarders, particularly Forest Service personnel, who were delighted to find this charming trio of ladies.

Red Fenwick, **DENVER POST** writer, wrote in 1954: "*Just past the Buckhorn Ranger Station and this side of the pass that gives you the first glimpse of the Mummy Range, you'll find the rambling log home of the Dickersons. You'll want to stop here and chat and meet the indomitable Dickersons. Silver-haired Mrs. Stella Dickerson, the mother, probably will be hoeing the garden or working on a painting. If you arrive during the fall months, you may have to scout around to find the ladies, because they will be busy as beaver. There is wood to be cut and stacked, supplies to be gathered and stored, canning to put up and many other preparations to be made for winter. And there are only Mrs. Dickerson and her two daughters to do it.*"

After the girls stopped working at the sawmill the three women went over to the Poudre Canyon one summer to work at Glen Echo. Dolly Stonemetz, Stella's cousin, owned Glen Echo at that time and badly needed their help, so they picked up their houseplants and away they went. Allen did not like that, but they

166

Glen Echo Resort.   *Miller photo, date unknown.*

did not feel guilty because he had help at his sawmill, Bradford Ramsey and Fred Grable. But leaving the hard sawmill labor to work at Glen Echo was like jumping from the frying pan into the fire. Stella worked in the kitchen; Helen and Alice in the dining room. Not only were they "hashslingers", but Dolly required them to do everything else, too....like washing clothes, cleaning cabins, pumping gas and baking cakes. They worked sixteen hours every day from May until September 1st.

*Inside Glen Echo.
Miller photo,
date unknown.*

They were so tired and worn out when they got home that Alice flaked out on the now-3'-high unkempt grass, gazed happily up at the sky and proclaimed, "Doesn't it feel good to lie down in the grass and do nothing? Look at the sun! Look at the sky! Listen to the birds! Doesn't this feel good?" They all three had hated the Glen Echo experience and did not regret one minute being away from there. It was, indeed, good to be home. Never again would they take on something like that. Even in later years

167

No place like home.   *Photo by Alice Dickerson, 1985.*

as recent as a month before she died, Helen said, shaking her head, "I was never as glad to get away from a place as I was from there. It was a terrible experience."

There was always something challenging for Alice and Helen to do in their "spare time". They gathered hundreds of bushels of lodgepole pine cones for Ranger Shorty Hughes in 1963. The Forest Service took truckloads of the cones to a Forest Service nursery in Monument, Colorado where they planned to plant 131,000 seedlings.

Technically, three-fourths of the cones were provided by squirrels who had already harvested those that were seed-bearing and buried them in underground caches. People were hastily told not to be stressed out about that. Squirrel diets are not limited to cones; they also store wild mushrooms, kinnikinnick berries and other forest goodies, necessary because of the uneven evergreen cone-producing years. In addition, if a collector took only part of his cache, the squirrel would happily fill it up again. But if she took all the cones, the squirrel would get discouraged and disappear. So it was a 50-50 contribution: score humans 50, squirrels 50.

At Monument, the cones were unsealed by soaking in warm water. Then they were air-dried and tumbled by a churn to thresh out the seeds. They were then tested for viability and stored in seed banks. Some were sent to other areas and others were planted in seed beds to start little trees for reforesting. Those planted in seed beds were plowed loose by machines after 24 months when they were about 10" tall. They were collected, bundled in bales of 2000 and either replanted for root conditioning or left in cold storage for National Forest orders.

Unfortunately, this interesting occupation was short-lived, because the nursery caretakers were found dead in their cabin one day and the project was moved elsewhere or abandoned.

The Bird Bander

Alice loved birds and read many words--
About them she learned what she could;
She fed them each day so they'd not go away
And made homes for them out of wood.
Dr. Ryder one day came to see her array
And to teach her all about banding;
One thousand or more was her netting score—
The professor was proud of her handling.

In the early sixties Alice became a bird banding sub-permitee of Dr. Ronald A. Ryder, a Wildlife Biology professor at Colorado State University. She obtained both federal and state banding permits. Dr. Ryder heard about Alice from some of the U.S. Forest Service personnel, who told him she was good with birds. He drove up, talked to her about banding, gave her some bands, traps and nets and taught her how to catch birds. Dr. Ryder himself began banding birds in 1949 as a graduate student and has continued even into his retired life.

"I banded birds of all kinds probably about ten years, more than sixty species of them," said Alice. "They came back for years. That's what banding is for...to tell how many years they come back, how long they live, etc. I banded at least one hundred hummingbirds, fifteen in one day once. Hummingbird numbers were so tiny you almost had to use a magnifying glass to see what they were. I banded nearly one thousand birds."

"With her sister Helen's assistance, Alice banded most of her birds right in their yard up the Buckhorn," said Dr. Ryder."Most of the species Alice banded were typical 'feeder birds' for that elevation: three woodpecker species, both black-capped and mountain chickadees, four races of juncos which were then considered separate species and are now 'lumped' as one species, twelve species of native sparrows and finches. She also trapped and banded tanagers, thrushes, thrashers, cowbirds, nuthatches, jays, robins, wrens, vireos, warblers and flycatchers."

According to Dr. Ryder, probably the most unusual birds banded were three species of hummingbirds totaling over one hundred, and common nighthawks, all caught in large, almost invisible Japanese nets used by ornithologists to catch birds for banding purposes known as "mistnets".

Alice regularly submitted first arrival dates each year, many of which were published in ***The Ptarmigan***, the monthly newsletter of the Fort Collins Audubon Society, and some in ***American Birds***, a magazine of the National Audubon Society.

Dr. Ryder was able to get many closeup photos of various bird species showing trapping and handling techniques and sex and age criteria at Alice's banding site.

"Although Alice recaptured many of her bandings, especially hummers and finches, over a period of years," recalled Dr. Ryder, "no distant recoveries were received to indicate summer or winter homes of migrants."

Through the banding experience, Alice gained valuable knowledge of birds and their habits. One time she told the professor that nighthawks eat plaster board. When he expressed disbelief, she told him to "come up and see." He went up and, sure enough, they were eating plaster board.

Helen did not care for nighthawks. One time she was holding one and it hissed at her and she could smell its breath. She told Alice, "Hurry up and band this thing; it has halitosis."

Alice stopped banding mainly because it became increasingly difficult to read the numbers on the tiny bands, particularly those of the hummingbirds.

Hummingbird in mist net.   *Ron Ryder photo.*

Ranch Life Variety

The eyes shone bright in the night car light—
  Alice stopped the car so they could see;
The bobcat hissed a threat, but it's a pretty safe bet
  She didn't get out 'til he dodged behind a tree.
The fawn, hardly touched, they threw in the truck
  And hauled it home to feed to all the crew.
It made the bobcat mad, but the sisters said "too bad;
  We'll eat the meat and try not to think of you."

The girls always enjoyed repeating the age-old saying, "Money doesn't grow on trees," then laugh and say that most of how they earned a living did: poles and posts, sawmilling, collecting pine cones, making Christmas wreaths, pine needle baskets......

Stella Dickerson was an inspiration to her daughters to try their hands at creative arts. Stella herself was a fine artist; when

Painting by Stella.   *Photo courtesy of Alice Dickerson.*

she was a school youngster, her teacher encouraged her by telling her that her talents lay in her fingers. She, of course, was extremely busy with her household chores, especially when she was feeding boarders, which was often, so she did not have a lot of time to pursue creative artwork. After telling her daughters for years she would save her serious painting for her old age, her eyesight in later years prevented her from following through on that promise; she was almost blind. She did, however, make rag rugs, but not with the use of her eyes. But the paintings she did complete, mostly watercolor and chalk drawings, were treasured by Alice and Helen and have always hung on the walls in their house as monuments to their mother's artistic skill.

During the years following Earl's death, Helen filled the shelves of the little stand with pine needle baskets of all sizes and shapes, skillfully and intricately fashioned.

Pine needle baskets of various sizes and shapes.
*Photo by Red Fenwick, the **Denver Post**, 1954.*

She and Alice made beautiful flower arrangements, the flowers having been pressed in sand so their shapes and colors looked like fresh bouquets mounted and framed. Mrs. Dickerson and her daughters entered some of their beautiful creations, including their home-baked bread, in fairs and hobby shows and became well-known in Larimer County.

Alice became quite adept at painting, most often of animals,

*Homemade light bread. Photo by Mildred Camp, **Loveland Reporter-Herald**, 1973.*

particularly elk, and her collages were especially well done and in much demand. Helen sliced deer and elk antlers for bolo ties and Alice painted the tiny animals on them. They made ladies' jewelry, toothpick holders and Alice made diminutive hummingbirds from pine cones, bread, balsa wood, glue, pins and fishline.

Collage by Alice Dickerson, 1973.

Earle Wilson, in a *Fort Collins Triangle Review* article, wrote: *"There was one memorable painting. It was a wonderfully-done oil landscape of a small lake with driftwood, clouds and pine trees with a marvelous background of craggy mountains. There was a narrow dirt road in the immediate foreground spanning the length of the painting. There were animal tracks on the road."*

"I finished it and laid it on the table for the oil to set," Alice

said, *"but I didn't lay it upside down. During the night a mouse got on the painting and 'walked' down the road leaving what looked like wolf tracks in the oil. I thought it was an interesting touch so I left them on the road."*

"She was right; the tracks took nothing from the painting," laughed Earle.

Alice did not participate in Helen's "stand" project, except to make paintings and toothpick holders, etc. for Helen to sell; she was too busy with everything else to bother with it. She did haul pop, candy, groceries and whatever else was not delivered from town.

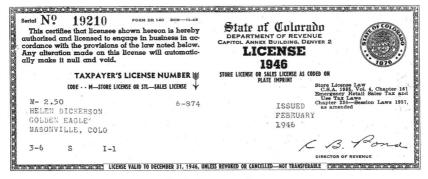

Helen's business license.

Helen worked very hard on crafts to sell, all year long. Alice made paintings only in fall and winter, "because if I mixed the oil up in spring and summer I'd have to throw it out because I wouldn't get to use it."

Until she got a generator, Helen had sanded all wood items by

Helen's studio where generator was kept.

hand; then she could use power tools, which made her craft work much easier.

Alice, a southpaw, was beginning to sustain some permanent injuries. Always, if she fell, she landed on her left knee. Then she injured her right shoulder when she fell while running one day.

Once in awhile Alice got off to do a little fishing. She fished for fun and always brought some home for Helen and her mother. When her cousins Ethyl and Larry Lomer came up from Denver, she fished with them.

Alice and her catch. Photo by Erwin D. Sias, 1960.

Alice once appeared at the breakfast table at 8 a.m., a very late breakfast hour at the Dickersons'. Her cousins jeered, "My, you're lazy." Alice, annoyed because she had been hoeing the garden since 4 a.m., snapped at the really lazy ones, "I've already done a day's work, where have you been ?" And she worked the rest of the day, albeit a little disgruntled.

During World War II Dick Lass, who had been foreman of the road work between the Lazy D and Rockwell Ranches in the 1920s, boarded with the Dickersons. He was building the road up

Cousin Ethyl's house.

Cascade Creek to the Ballard place for the timber sale and fire access after the Forest Service had acquired his release from the shipyards in California. Dick told the Dickersons that working in the shipyards was like being under a big metal tub with hammers pounding on it.

Another boarder, Bill Thurston, who sometimes was accompanied by his wife, core-drilled for beryl on Crystal Mountain in 1948 and found some good sites. He said Crystal Mountain is one of about a dozen beryl-rich pegmatite areas in Larimer County. He considered this important because there was a big demand for beryl during World War II.

While gas rationing was in force during the war, a woman stopped in her car hunting help for her burned husband. The Dickerson ladies invited them in and got some dry clothes for the injured man while Allen ran to get him some new trousers. The ladies medicated his burns and packed him in blankets until he was over the chills and shock. They listened to his story:

He had tried to start a fire across the pass at Bennett Creek with paper and kindling, but it would not burn. He went to the car, got his can of rationed gas and threw some on the kindling, thinking there was no fire there. But...it exploded and caught his clothes on fire and his hands, face, neck and ears were badly burned. He jumped into the creek, icy with early spring runoff, so was chilled to the bone when they arrived at Dickersons'.

When he felt like returning to Greeley, Alice took her car and Allen drove the burned man's car over the worst of the rutty Buckhorn to a place where he decided he could drive all right. The next day his doctor said he had second degree burns, but he healed up without big scars. They returned with the borrowed clothes some time later.

One July 4th John Kitchen went down off Pennock Pass to the Dickersons to get his hand fixed. He had a little pole sale up there and his horse had run against a tree, jamming his hand between the singletree and the tree. The girls cleaned and doctored his ripped-open hand, a bloody mess. He went back to work for two days, took his load out and went to the doctor, who gave him an O.K. and praised the Dickerson "doctors" for their fine work.

The girls had been to a school program one night down at Masonville and were on their way home. It was late. Seeing some glaring eyes at the side of the road, they stopped. Alice got out and, with flashlight in hand, jumped back as a loud hiss greeted her in a not-too-friendly tone. She pointed the light at the hissing creature and discovered it to be an irate bobcat that had just killed a half-grown deer fawn. The cat ran off and the girls dressed the deer, threw it into the truck and took it home. They all had some very tender venison to eat, thanks to the hapless bobcat.

After her father was gone, Alice still trapped some, but she quit about 1944 for good. She did not want to trap anymore and did not want anyone else to, either. She just did not have the heart for it; she had always loved wildlife and now that trapping was not a necessity, she gladly stopped.

A plane crashed on Crystal Mountain in summer, 1951. When they were hunting for the plane, one car of newsmen stopped at Dickersons' on their way to Pingree Park to inquire as to the whereabouts of Hague's Peak. The three women finally convinced them the crash was on Crystal Mountain, not Hague's. Alice had just returned from a hike and had been watching planes circling one spot on that mountain. So, after consuming some delicious nourishment, the men proceeded to Crystal Mountain. All fifty of the plane's occupants had been killed. Two of the men working on the grisly aftermath of the wreck boarded at Dickersons. Coincidentally, Alice and Helen used to play with one of the crash victims when they visited Windsor as little girls.

John Derby always let his cattle run at the Dickersons'. "He always pretended like our place was his place," said Alice. "When we'd fix fence the cattle would 'bite' the fence in two. One day we got on our horses and took his cattle clear down the Buckhorn. We just went a-sailing down the road with them. Even jumped over the cattle guard. He didn't find them for three weeks." He said, "I wanted to brand those cattle and now I can't find them." To which Alice replied sharply, "Well then, don't put them on our place if you don't want them to be lost."

Helen acquired a reputation in Mummy country for being a skilled seamstress. She had a Singer treadle sewing machine and made fifteen dresses on it one year and a wedding dress for a young girl. Stella made Alice a dress out of new material once...green satin. Alice just loved that dress and marveled that her mother used the money to buy the material. She did it so Alice would look nice for a particular party.

Helen and Alice made hundreds of wreaths for several winters and sold part of them at Tolliver and Kenney in Fort Collins, also to Venango, Nebraska to Herb and Berdena Sattler, who in turn sold them to the Rainbow Girls for a money-making project. They sold many to individuals who went up especially to buy them. Alice said, "I got so I couldn't even enjoy Christmas. My hands would ache so I couldn't enjoy anything. I'd feel like my hands were going to sleep and I'd shake them to try to wake them up. I couldn't even sleep. We'd work out in the cold, sometimes zero,

Helen making a wreath.   *Photo by Alice, 1981.*

and pretty near freeze to death. Then get nothing. We only got $1.50 apiece for them. They were worth $20. We worked from October to pretty near Christmas, every year. We stored them in the chicken house and cellar; stacked hundreds of them everywhere we could get them. We'd have a whole pickup load of boxes to take down to the express and ship. Helen and I. Our hands were just ruined when we got through, but they were beautiful wreaths and year after year were in much demand."

One morning one of the cows came to the barn by herself without her calf. Helen went down to where the cow had been and found the calf dead. There were what appeared to be coyote tracks all around, so she went back to get Alice and some traps. When the two of them returned to the sad scene, the calf was gone. No drag marks, but tracks, which they followed and never did catch up with whatever was making them...it went over to the Buckhorn. The calf was carried, not dragged; for an animal to carry a newborn calf, it had to be large, like a wolf.

Ranger Stagleman called from Bennetts one evening and asked for supper, but he and the other rangers did not arrive until 9 p.m. Their pack mule had given them fits crossing the top of the pass and had brushed the pack off on a tree. They repacked; then the stubborn old cuss ran down the fence line instead of going through the gate at the top of Pennock Pass. They were a little worried when they arrived at Dickersons that they were too late for supper, but the consistently hospitable Dickerson ladies smiled and fed the hungry men their warmed-over, home-cooked supper.

Stella's Last Days

Stella, a fine wife, had a good life;
Through hardship she fared very well.
Her daughters were nice and lacking in vice;
Her good will and values never fell.
She taught the girls art, close to her heart,
Which characterized both of their lives.
Then when she died, the girls at her side,
They saddened, but for life were supplied.

While the timber sales were still in full swing at the head of Elk Creek in the upper Buckhorn, Alice, one late February day, looked toward Pennock Pass and said, "Isn't that smoke coming over the mountain?......I know it is! The flames are coming, too!" It was a very dry year and this particular day it was very warm with a west wind blowing, so it was a matter of grave concern to the Dickersons, who lay right in the path of the fire if it were to advance as far as their little ranch. Helen phoned the Forest Service in Fort Collins. They looked out and said they could see it, too. Meanwhile, one young fellow from the timber camp at the top of the pass started toward the Dickersons' on his horse, but the horse seemed to be in slow motion, so he jumped off and ran. When he arrived, he fell to the ground practically unconscious. The ladies thought he was having a heart attack or something, but he finally came out of it. To ease his anxiety, Allen informed him they had already reported the fire and the Forest Service was on their way. Several men gathered at the cabin waiting to go to the fire. While they were sitting on the ground, little ashes landed on them, still in the shape of pine needles. Alice shuddered when recalling it, and said, "It was scary." Fortunately that night it started snowing and the dry spell ended. They had lots of snow the rest of the winter and the springs were filled again.

Every winter day the Dickersons were busy, hauling in wood to keep fires going, shoveling snow, working on crafts, cooking, repairing, feeding birds and squirrels and doing all the other things they were too busy to do in the summer. Always there were visitors coming to chat and sip coffee while eating home-baked bread or cookies.

Helen broke her arm the last time she and Alice put up ice. A rock rolled out from under her foot enabling her and the block of

Helen, Stella and Alice busy at work.
*Photo by Red Fenwick, **Denver Post**, 1954.*

ice she was carrying to fall on her arm. From that time forward, they converted to Servel propane refrigerators and deep freezes.

There were quiet days, too, not only for the three ladies in their cozy cabin, but for Allen, across the meadow. One cold winter day Allen was looking out his window at a rabbit hopping  around in the snow. Suddenly the rabbit jumped high into the air with what appeared to be a piece of white paper clinging to its neck. On closer examination as the rabbit floundered in the snow, he recognized the "white paper" to be a weasel in its white winter coat performing its natural murderous thing.

Rarely a ptarmigan appeared, but only during a four or five foot snow. Most likely during those times the birds made a quick descent down from their winter home on the Mummy, searching for easier pickings. During one of the deep snows, Allen was riding the family horse to feed horses at the ranger station. A ptarmigan suddenly flew up from under him, providing the horse the opportunity to prove to Allen he could perform a high jump in place quite effectively.

Stella Dickerson became ill and the girls took care of her at home as long as they possibly could. Eventually an ambulance took her to the hospital in Ft. Collins. She passed away in 1964 and was buried alongside her husband in Fort Collins.

*Stella (1884-1964) and daughters Helen (L) and Alice (R). Photo by Red Fenwick, **Denver Post**, 1954.*

Stella had left an indelible impression on those who had met her; she was a lady and always displayed warm hospitality to everyone entering her primitive, but charming little home. Also, she must take much of the credit for bringing up two fine daughters who, like their mother, were loved by all who knew them and who displayed talents which she had encouraged. She also instilled in them frugality, generosity, kindness, diligence and a keen sense of right and wrong, among other fine qualities.

Stella learned to endure severe hardships in the harsh high-altitude Rocky Mountain climate and transferred that endurance gracefully to her daughters, who quietly accepted the rugged way of life not resignedly, but with firm, contented resoluteness.

VI.
THREE
"YOUNG'UNS" LEFT
1964-1971

Allen's cabin.

Bears and Crosses

The girls said, "Oh, dear, what's that we hear—
A scratching like somebody's boot!"
Helen ran to see who the intruder might be
While Alice got her gun to shoot;
Helen peered outside and frightened she cried,
"A bear! Right here! At our screen!"
With a resounding ring Alice shot the thing
And he wished he had never been seen.

Alice and Helen were now alone in the little cabin and their uncle Allen was alone across the way. All three persevered in their pursuits on the firmly-established homestead and people who stopped by, old friends and new, were beginning to really take notice of these rugged mountain people; they were becoming legends. Most people were changing their ways of living, buying new houses, all household adults earning salaries, buying recreational boats and vehicles and flowing with the waves of mainstream America. But the Dickerson sisters, as they now were being called, still lived in much the same way as they and their ancestors had always lived on the homestead, and they were doing it by their own choosing and were perfectly content. There was a fascination there from wave-riding mainstream people: a stability; a total lack of a desire for change to "keep up with the Joneses". Why, the Dickerson sisters are still baking bread from scratch in a wood stove! They have no electricity and no modern conveniences! And they don't mind! As Alice always said,

"We never had it, so we don't miss it."

One mid-afternoon during a Decoration Day weekend Alice and Helen heard a lot of racket on the east side of their house. Helen ran into her bedroom and found herself face to face with a big brown bear draped across the window, chewing and slobbering on the screen. She ran to close the shed door in an attempt to prevent the bear from entering the house. By that time it had retreated somewhat and was sitting on the bank outside the now-closed shed door. Then it got up, growled, and climbed up the tree by the shed. If it had wanted to terrify Helen, it accomplished its mission. Alice came with her .410 shotgun and, to scare it, shot it in the nose. She, too, accomplished her mission, because the bear hauled down that tree in jig time and, according to sources at the ranger station, came hustling in there, scaring off the horses and, of all things, a pet cat. The girls did not know how it missed stopping at the stand; it would have had a heyday as the shutters were open and it was loaded with candy bars.

A young man knocked on the sisters' door a cold day in December, 1966. He told them he needed water for his vehicle and that he had left his friend up on the hill with his sick girlfriend. The ladies gave him some water and Alice said, "It's cold. Zero. I'll give you a cap to put on your head." Soon a car pulled up and, when Helen opened the door, one of the two men held a gun to her face and said, "We won't hurt you if you give us what we want." Alice related, "They had binder twine in their pockets and they tied us hand and foot and made us lie on the floor and tied our hands behind our backs. Trussed us up like turkeys. They demanded money. We had to give it to them or they would have shot us. The Least of the Evils said, 'let's go.' The Other Evil said, 'I'm going to look around.' They left, drove over the pass, which was open that year and we got loose. I locked the door and Helen called the sheriff. The Evils broke through roadblocks, but finally got caught. They had broken into other places besides us. We got our money back and the Evils spent a lot of time in prison. It was a terrible experience for us. We never kept money around home again."

Jack Greer, of Bellvue, began harvesting the Dickerson hay crop. Jack owned cattle, so needed the hay. Helen and Alice no

Jack Greer baling hay.   *Alice Dickerson photo, 1981.*

longer had livestock, so there was no need for them to keep hay; now it was a welcome source of income for the sisters.

Visitors came often and the sisters were always glad to see them, no matter how busy they were. An exchange of news was most often part of the visit; thus Alice and Helen always were up on what was going on in their surrounding habitat, country and world.

One day, while sipping coffee and munching on homemade cookies, some Forest Service men complained to the ladies that someone was tearing down their White Pine Mountain signs. To satisfy their curiosity, Alice, Helen and some friends hiked up there one day and, sure enough, the first sign was ripped and scarred with deep grooves. Upon closer examination and her usual thorough scrutiny, Alice declared, "Here is some black bear hair on the tree; that's what has been tearing up this sign."

Anyone who knew Alice Dickerson never doubted her word; she always had a remarkable memory and a reputation for being right at least 95% of the time.

One day a CSU truck with trailer went by the house and Alice said, "That looks like a bear trap on that trailer." It was, but they did not see the bear in it. On the way back the truck driver stopped to see the girls and told them they had caught the bear being a garbage pest at the CSU Forestry Camp. They took it up to Cascade Creek, spilled some paint on it for future identification purposes and turned it loose.

The Masonville Church congregation asked Alice and Helen if they would make a cross for the church and told them how they wanted it made. Alice recalled the history of the cross.

"Helen and I cut the log one morning when we were on our way to Fort Collins to do our shopping. Miss Elizabeth Geiger had said we could have a cedar log if we wanted to make the bottoms of baskets. The cedar was about the color of the pine needles and made the baskets prettier. We were dressed up and on the way to town in our 1939 Chevrolet pickup. I knew where a cedar log was...across the creek lying on the ground. To get there we jumped from stone to stone trying to stay dry. We cut into the log to make sure it wasn't rotten. It was already cured so we cut the one-foot diameter log into a six-foot length just long enough to fit in the back of the pickup with a one-man crosscut saw. We carried it across the creek still trying to stay dry and clean and loaded it in the pickup. It was so massive that it drew quite a bit of attention

Masonville Church cross made by Helen and Alice. Photo by Reverend Vic Urban, 1993.

in downtown Fort Collins. People looked inquisitively at it, then looked away with almost signboard thoughts painted on their faces which read, what are those women doing with that log in their truck. But we had killed three birds with one stone; found a suitable log for the cross, stayed clean and dry for errands in town and saved gas. The boards were sawed by our uncle Allen with an old steam engine saw-mill at the end of our garden. We sanded it by hand because we couldn't plane for fear of chipping it. It was a hard job. Helen chipped and grooved the boards so they fit tight, then sanded them smooth and put the emblem on it. We cut the emblem with a fret saw with a hair sized blade."

The Timnath Church wanted one of the beautiful crosses, too, so the girls obliged.

Uncle Allen

Allen could shoot a stem off of fruit--
  His vision was eagle keen.
His trade was sawed boards; he drove Model T Fords-
  Made shingles the best ever seen.
But he hardly knew whatever to do
  With sweet-smelling soap night or day.
He lived all alone, kept in touch with a phone
  With his nieces 'cross the field of hay.

Allen had been a heavy smoker, but when the doctor told him to either quit or die, he quit and lived seven more years, but was afflicted with emphysema. He had a huge, enlarged heart and became quite despondent when he became sick with the disease. After his father died, he had sawed wood on the porch until it was almost impossible to get in and out of the house. Finally, he moved from Grandpa's house over to the cabin. Alice cleaned Sam's porch and put 2x6s across it so people could walk without plunging, tripping or falling through.

Allen's Cabin.

Alice had always liked Allen, though he infuriated her sometimes; he was always teasing her. He loved to hunt, so Alice would buy him his license and take him in her pickup, her binoculars close by.

He had incredible vision. One time when they were out hunting he said, "I see a deer." Alice took the glass and, sure enough, there, about a mile away, stood a deer, and he had seen it without the glass. He did not shoot at it, of course, because of the great distance.

Much to Alice's and Helen's chagrin, Allen up and sold the crank telephone, still in the ladies' house, to Jake Lowery for five dollars. When he was questioned about this sudden action, he said it was because he had been told the telephones soon were to be changed to more modern ones by the telephone company, which the company did, but not soon.

Allen installed a World War II telephone system from his house to the girls' so they could call back and forth. But eventually he could not even handle that, so Alice would go up and check to see if he was all right, because if she did not hear him on the phone, she was afraid she would find him dead. He had threatened to kill himself and had told the doctor he had a gun.

Alice took care of him when he was sick until a day or two before he died. The last winter of his life, she took him to the doctor every week when she could. Sometimes she and Helen had to do a lot of shoveling to get through.

Allen Dickerson passed away in 1971 in the Loveland hospital and was buried in Windsor alongside his parents, Sam and Cora Dickerson.

Allen Dickerson 1897-1971.   *Photographer unknown, 1965.*

The Dickerson sisters were truly alone now; the rest of the seven original homestead family were gone. Sometimes, while Helen was working at her stand, people would ask, when looking around at several abandoned cabins, "Do you know anything about this ghost town?" And Helen, with her usual good sense of humor, would reply, "I'm one of the original ghosts!"

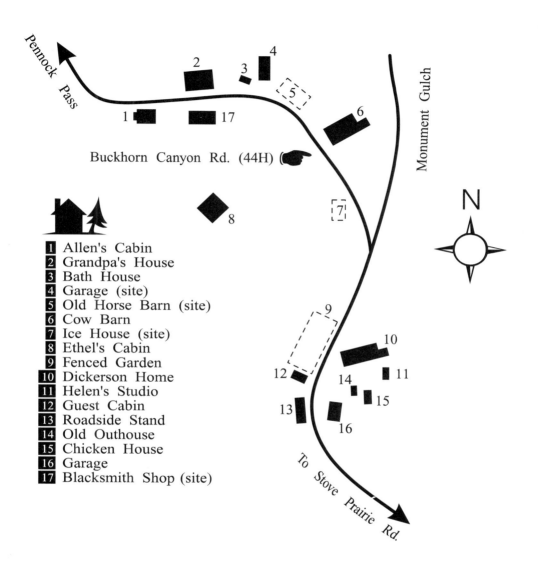

Pennock Pass

2

3

4

5

1

17

Buckhorn Canyon Rd. (44H)

6

Monument Gulch

8

7

N

1 Allen's Cabin
2 Grandpa's House
3 Bath House
4 Garage (site)
5 Old Horse Barn (site)
6 Cow Barn
7 Ice House (site)
8 Ethel's Cabin
9 Fenced Garden
10 Dickerson Home
11 Helen's Studio
12 Guest Cabin
13 Roadside Stand
14 Old Outhouse
15 Chicken House
16 Garage
17 Blacksmith Shop (site)

9

10

11

12

14

15

13

16

To Stove Prairie Rd.

Dickerson Ranch Buildings.

VII
THE
SISTERS ALONE
1971-1992

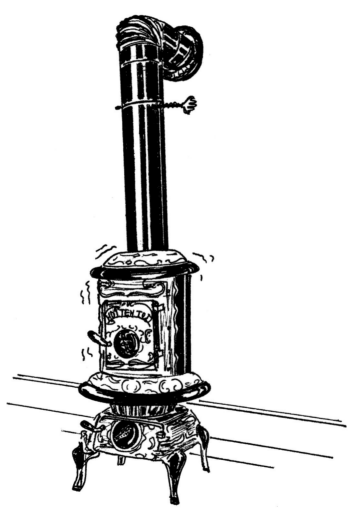

The sitting room stove.

The Dickerson Sisters

Helen and Alice were kin without malice—
As close as two sisters could be;
They stood by each other after losing their mother—
A splendor for all to see.
When one saw a need, the other agreed
And they shared in most every chore.
For the rest of their days they retained their ways
And their friends loved to enter their door.

After Allen died, Alice and Helen were fire wardens in their districts. But they ended up just pulling out stranded cars...nothing else. Being fire wardens had become a family tradition; first Earl, then Allen and now the sisters. Alice took the fire warden sign down off their front yard post and said, "take it away". Instead of

coordinating fire-fighting efforts, they were actually running the Upper Buckhorn Canyon Towing Service, and they didn't like it. They took their shovels and dug out car after car——themselves, while the inexperienced, foolhardy drivers watched. The Forest Service did not like their attitude, but the Forest Service wasn't pulling and digging out cars.

Alice laughed when talking about the electricity they used to have: "Helen's generator she used for sanding I used occasionally for TV. If we had company, we had an electric light over the kitchen table. It was a beautiful light. One time one of the Masonville folks called and asked if they could have a surprise birthday party for Katherine Cross; seven of them were coming up. They packed a picnic basket with nothing in it and told her they were having a picnic up on the pass. When they got here, I told Katherine the party is here, not up there. She said, 'What?' and we had the nicest party under the electric light over the kitchen table. They couldn't believe it."

Helen was still operating the stand, but she tired of making antler jewelry, because it bothered her hip to pull the cord on the generator engine. Sometimes she had to wind and wind to get it going. She had cut the antlers by hand and sanded them with her generator-powered sander, but it got to be more than she could handle.

Helen cutting antlers for jewelry. Photo by Alice Dickerson, October, 1980.

She also began losing her vision. She could not see to attach the little cut out pictures around which she painted little backgrounds, so she quit making them. Alice, still with eagle vision, painted the little pictures on those she made.

Helen did have an unusual sales approach, although it did not hurt her business. "When it gets too busy," she laughed, when talking to a ***Loveland Daily Reporter-Herald*** reporter, "and I don't have enough time for myself, I just lock up the stand and go on up to the house."

They never charged enough for their beautiful creations- $6 to $10 for pine needle baskets, each taking at the least a minimum of 16 hours to make. Tourists from all over the world bought their artistic pieces, many who began correspondence with the ladies

after returning home. Then modern America began entering the area. Menacing remarks or threats from strange men were spoiling the easygoing, friendly and trusting atmosphere at the stand. Alice warned, "Why don't you get rid of the thing and maybe we can sell more things at the house. Like baskets. You aren't making anything on the stuff you buy to sell."

Helen had made candy to sell, but now she was not allowed to make it, so she had to buy it. "Pure Foods Law. Health Department said she couldn't do it without two sinks and I said, let's forget it. I said it would be all right to sell a pop can that a dog

Helen's baskets.   *Photographer unknown, 1960s.*

197

lifted his leg on, but you couldn't sell the stuff that you made," Alice said, bitterly. "No one was cleaner making candy than Helen."

One year, the day before the 4th of July, someone broke into the stand and took all the candy, pop, gum and cigarettes. Souvenirs were all Helen had left. In 1973 Helen closed the stand. It was no longer safe for her to be in there alone meeting the "public." But she kept making baskets even until a few days before her death years later.

Helen's stand closed forever.

Theirs is a beautiful valley, with coyotes, elk, Abert squirrels and deer frequenting the area around them. Alice enjoyed walking four miles to fish or gather moss for her dish gardens. The sisters were never lonely, as their days were filled with a healthy combination of necessary chores and creative activity. Visitors have always been amazed at how the girls complemented each other while performing tasks. Each always knew what the other was doing...an example of genuine teamwork.

Teamwork by Alice and Helen. Basket courtesy of Jane Wallower. Photo by Elyse Bliss, 1993.

The girls became used to their propane lights, refrigerator, deep freeze and a two-burner stove and gave up ever having electricity.

"It would be nice to have," said Alice, "but when poles were being run in, the cost was too high to even consider. If the ranger station had paid to have electricity, we would have gotten it for quite a bit less, because the poles would have had to come right by here, but they didn't want to pay the $1000 a pole, either. But it's hard to miss what you've never had."

When the generator was going, Alice enjoyed watching her black and white TV, but Helen did not really care.

"One time I was in the middle of watching this bull fight," said Alice, not smiling. "Helen was in the shed polishing some antlers, and when she was finished, she shut off the generator."

"Alice never did find out who won the bull fight," Helen laughed. "We could still have the generator, but we'd have to ask someone to haul gas up here and we don't want to do that. It's not that important."

The sisters were entertaining Mr.and Mrs.Lowery one beautiful sunny summer evening in 1982. He was a fire patrol aide for the Forest Service and they lived down at the ranger station. There was only one cloud in the sky. Alice was seated at the kitchen table under the water pipes on the ceiling. Helen and the Lowerys were seated around the room. Suddenly they saw a big ball of fire go over Alice's head, down to the faucet and into the drain.

"It was the most horrible explosion I've ever heard in my life; sounded like an atomic bomb went off," Alice said. "All in one clap thunder and lightning. Bang! A terrific crash. Nobody was hurt, but they said I looked like a ghost. I ended up with a headache and didn't feel good. My eyes were queer-looking and red."

Lightning-struck fallen tree and sisters.Photographer unknown, 1968.

In less than an instant it was over. They surveyed the damage. In the front room the thunderbolt neatly removed some of the wallpaper. The useless main telephone was not touched, but the Army field telephone, on a doily on an enamel table, was ruined. The enamel was burned, but the doily was untouched. A full-length bedroom mirror was blown into one inch pieces which were scattered everywhere. They checked the cellar and found lids loosened on eleven cans of fruit....huckleberries and other kinds. Outside, eleven trees were struck at once, one which had been hit before, which relegates to an old wives' tale the belief that lightning never strikes the same place twice. One tree about eighty yards from the house was split wide open and half of it fell to the ground during the night several hours after the lightning struck, which, of course, brought both

Helen and Alice straight up out of bed without much delay. The falling tree had narrowly missed the northeast corner of the cabin. Under one big tree a Union Leader tobacco can was struck beneath a pile of wood. A hole was torn in it about the size of a dime.

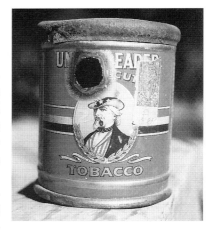

Union Leader tobacco can with lightning hole. Photo by Elyse Bliss, 1993.

Everything smelled like sulphur. Someone said it must have been cold lightning, or it would have burned everything up. Alice said, "I'd hate for it to be any hotter." It was an experience none of them hoped to repeat....ever.

Another day, the same summer, a terrible hailstorm pounded the little cabin unmercifully, splitting their 50-year-old homemade lodgepole pine shingles. The hailstones were huge, "as big as hen eggs", and when the storm finished, shingles were lying all over the ground.

Sometimes when Mr. Lowery was not at home, Mrs. Lowery would go up and eat dinner with the girls. He did not want her to walk up by herself, so Alice would meet her halfway. One evening Alice heard something in the bushes and, believing it was a wild turkey or some other creature, she waited to see what. Soon a bobcat appeared. Alice, talented in many ways, was known for her perfect imitation of a domestic cat spitting, so she spit beautifully at the bobcat, but it laid back its ears and just sat there looking at her, so she decided to move on and not wait for him to formulate definite plans. She met Mrs. Lowery and on the way back the cat had disappeared; he had made his plans apparently and, like Alice, it was a decision to move on.

Alice consented to make some collages, write a history of the area and check on the ranger station during the winter for the Forest Service. She made several collages, including one of the ranger station, which are still hung in Forest Service offices in Fort Collins. These assignments were in about 1977-79. She went down to the station about three times a week to check all the buildings and locks to see if there was any vandalism or break-ins. Sometimes she found disturbances and called the Forest Service to tell them they had better come up and check into it. She and

One of Alice's collages made for the U.S. Forest Service.
Photo by Elyse Bliss.

Helen worked on the historical notes the entire winter of 1977.

When rangers did stay up during the winter months they used generators for electricity. Formerly they had used propane. However, those in charge had been worried about accidents because many different employees were using the ranger station facilities, increasing the possibility that some might not have sufficient knowledge to use it. So they took practically new propane refrigerators out to the dump. Later they regretted the wasteful action, or said they did, because someone else could have used them.

When the Lowerys were still at the ranger station, Helen (Lowery), a 7th Day Adventist, persuaded Alice to take evening Bible study. They told both Helen and Alice that if they studied the whole Bible they would give them each a diploma and Bible. Alice studied it four times from cover to cover. The teachers came up to the ranger station and gave tests for several months. The ladies each received what they had been promised for their efforts. Church activity was not new to the sisters; they had attended church regularly as children with their mother in Masonville while they were going to school. They seldom, if ever, went to church from home, because of the long distance to travel and, most importantly, no means of travel.

A man named Mark Horvat visited the Dickerson sisters in the 70s. He came not just for a visit but to talk shingles with them. Explaining that he had been employed as District Forester for Larimer and Weld Counties, he told them he was now eager to go into business for himself making pine shake shingles. He told them he had noticed that many of the older house, cabin and barn roofs in his area were made of native lodgepole pine rather than conventional red cedar shake shingles. He went on to tell them that he had researched this quite extensively and discovered that the pine shakes had been milled by the Dickerson family until 1952.

"Yes," nodded the ladies, "that's true."

Horvat told them he was convinced that he could produce an economical, high quality shingle well-suited to the area's dry climate. But, he added, he needed a recommendation from them so he could saw the shingles. Alice and Helen related to him that their cabin had those shingles for about fifty years; then the hailstorm had hit.

"The hailstones were the size of hen eggs," said Alice. "Those huge things split them. So we had to get regular rolled roofing. That stuff is nothing compared to those lodgepole shingles. They are the best. You've got your recommendation from us."

He told them he wished he had known they had trouble; he would have given them enough shingles to roof their house. Horvat spent three years convincing the building code inspectors his proposed product was economical, more wearable and historical. Eventually he won local approval from every community along the Front Range from Fort Collins to Pueblo and named his enterprise "Needmor Forestry."

Associate professor of Wood Science and Technology at Colorado State University, Harry Troxell, said, "*Lodgepole pine will wear much better than western red cedar in the Fort Collins area because it is denser. The higher density makes the shingles more resistant to hail damage. In this dry climate decay, the usual reason a wood roof must be replaced, is rarely, if ever, a problem.*"

Horvat began making his pine shake shingles in 1982. Ironically, houses, barns and other buildings all over the Front Range are capped with Dickerson-style shingles. All but the Dickersons' very own cabin.

The Dickerson home.

The Weather Reporter

She kept track every day of exactly the way
The weather was cloudy or clear;
If it rained or was hot, it did not escape plot
On the chart every month of the year.
She melted the snow so she would know
Amounts of moisture produced in each storm;
Her records on thunder were clearly no blunder—
So tickled with them was Wirshborn.

Alice had, for several years, been reporting weather on a volunteer basis to the Office of Civil Defense and the National Weather Service through the U.S. Forest Service. Her name, therefore, appeared on the Civil Defense list of volunteers when the 100-year Big Thompson flood took place on July 31, 1976.

Jim Wirshborn obtained the list of Civil Defense volunteers after that flood and wrote to Alice, as she had no phone, asking if she would be a volunteer weather reporter for him at Mountain States Weather Services. Alice obliged in the summer of 1977 and faithfully kept daily weather records for him. Jim gave her charts on which she could keep the records. Steve Babcoke, who used to bring up their recharged radio batteries, picked up the records every other week and took them down to Ft. Collins. Otherwise, she sent them in. She checked the weather, how much snow or rain, how much water there was in the snow, temperature, wind, etc. She could not obtain wind velocity because she did not have the proper instrument. Jim Wirshborn said that Alice's reports are one of the longest continuous records he has. He also said, "Alice has kept beautiful records on thunder, the best I have."

Alice was still reporting to Jim in 1993; she was a valuable reporter for him because few, if any, people live at that high altitude all year long.

MOUNTAIN STATES WEATHER SERVICES
Serving the Rocky Mountain West

STATION East side Research Park
TIME OF REGULAR OBSERVATION 9 AM
MONTH June YEAR 93

RECORD OF DAILY WEATHER OBSERVATIONS

DATE	24 HR HI TEMP	24 HR LO TEMP	TEMP AT OBSN.	AMOUNT OF PRECIPITATION (IN)	AMOUNT OF SNOWFALL (IN)	AMOUNT OF SNOW / ICE ON GROUND	TIME OF PRECIPITATION OCCURRENCE	WEATHER DAYS A B C D E F G H I	REMARKS	DATE
1									wet sky - all	1
2										2
3	50	40	40	trace	0	0		X	Cloudy	3
4	60	50	38	fog	0	0		X	Cloudy	4
5	60	50	58	0	0	0			Cloudy	5
6	60	60	58		0	0		X	Part Cloudy	6
7	70	36	36		0	0			Part Cloudy	7
8	50	50	40		0	0		X	Raining	8
9	50	40	45	0	0	0	X		Clear yet	9
10	60	32	60	0	0	0			Cloudy	10
11	60	40	40	0	0	0			Part Cloudy	11
12	70	40	60	0	0	0			Clear	12
13	70	40	70	0	0	0			Part Cloudy	13
14	73	35	70	0	0	0			Part Cloudy	14
15	70	40	70	0	0	0			Part Cloudy	15
16	70	40	70	0	0	0			Part Cloudy	16
17	50	40	70	.44	0	0	X		raining	17
18	45	40	41	.54	0	0	X X		raining	18
19	70	35	56	0	0	0			raining	19
20	73	40	40	.06	0	0	X X		rainy yet	20
21	76	40	60	0	0	0	X		clear yet	21
22	70	40	40	0	0	0	X		Part Cloudy	22
23	60	35	40	0	0	0	X		Part Cloudy	23
24	70	30	40	0	0	0	X		Part Cloudy	24
25	60	40	40	0	0	0	X		Part Cloudy	25
26	60	43	40	0	0	0	X		Part Cloudy	26
27	60	40	60	0	0	0	X		fair	27
28	60	40	65	0	0	0	X		fog	28
29	60	40	50	0	0	0			fog windy	29
30										30
31										31
TOTAL										TOTAL
AVG.				MAX.		DATE				

Special observations, notes and supplementary precipitation measurements: _____

MAIL COMPLETED FORMS TO: Mountain States Weather Services
904 E. Elizabeth St.
Fort Collins, Colorado 80524

REPORT SEVERE WEATHER IMMEDIATELY TO
(303) 224-9192
ALL OTHER CALLS
(303) 484-WIND

Weather Days:
A. Lt. Fog D. Sleet G. Duststorm
B. Hvy. Fog E. Hail H. Haze/Smoke
C. Thunder F. Glaze I. Blwg. Snow

OBSERVER Alice Dickerson

MSWS Form F-16
Rvsd. March 1, 1987

The Telephone Fiasco

The boys cutting pine let the trees hit the line;
  Now the sisters were alone without a phone.
The girls said they'd buy, but the ranger couldn't lie,
  Said "I'm sorry, but our law is carved in stone."
Alice fixed the break but that, too, was a mistake,
  So the girls proceeded to tear the line down.
He said you can't do that, the girls said drat!
  (And the poles made the best fenceposts around.)

For awhile the Dickersons enjoyed having a telephone and could be like real world people and call other real world people. But whoever bought the timber in Monument Gulch sometime in the 70s tore the telephone line down, which put the sisters back in the Great Mountain Cavewomen Days again. Jo Smethurst, a friend, tried her better-than-best to get the phone line reinstated. Following are some excerpts from some of the correspondence related to the fiasco:

11-14-75

Dear Alice & Helen,
  I had a note from Fannon Thompson, a vice president of Southwest Bell and he is willing to subscribe if that would help clarify maintenance. He would be willing to pay $10.00 per month. He suggests a citizens' band radio if you lose the telephone line. It is not nearly as good, but would be better than nothing.
                    Jo Smethurst

12-18-75

Dear Mrs. Smethurst:
  Thank you for your letter of concern over the Monument Gulch telephone line which is owned and maintained by the Forest Service. I realize the phone service to the Dickerson sisters as well as to the ranger station has been invaluable at times. Also, they have given very useful assistance to the Poudre District which would not have been possible without the telephone or some other form of communication.

As I view the phone line situation at this time, a number of alternatives are possible:

1. Retain the phone line in its present status to be maintained by the Forest Service or others. Regardless of who maintained the line, a safety hazard would exist.

2. Remove the phone line and have Forest Service radio contact with Buckhorn Work Center. This would save Forest Service maintenance money and would eliminate any direct line of communications for Helen and Alice Dickerson during the summer months.

3. Remove the phone line and install a radio-telephone at the Buckhorn Work Center—hopefully with a link to the Dickerson house. This would be cheaper than the phone line maintenance as F.S. would only pay for the radio the months it is in use.

There are other alternatives. It is my intention to continue with the past policy of lending a portable radio to Helen and Alice when one is available (generally winter).

James W. Carson
District Ranger

11-24-76

Dear Ladies:

Because the line serving you is on Forest Service land, it is a service station line and any maintenance that must be performed will have to be done by the Forest Service itself. Because you are the only parties on the line other than the Forest Service work center they will provide you with a radio for emergency service which will aid you this winter.

Peter A. Letourneau
Public Utilities Commission

12-7-76

To John Cormack, Mountain States T & T Co.:

I am writing in reference to 6 miles of telephone line that is situated between the Little South Fork road of the Poudre via Monument Gulch Road #35 East to Alice and Helen Dickerson and the Buckhorn Ranger Station. This phone line was established in 1913 which the Dickerson family helped build and apparently is a Forest Service line and has been out since 10-17. Is there any way this telephone line could be saved? This is very critical and I must stress critical.

Alice and Helen Dickerson's folks homesteaded in 1911 and have lived on the upper Buckhorn on the east side of Pennock Pass all these years. Their parents died several years ago, so the ladies have relied on usage of the phone. No one knows the harassment caused by people stopping and wanting to break into some of their

*buildings and they are many miles from help of the Sheriff's Depart-
ment, people wanting to use the phone for auto accidents, many,
many breakdowns or being stuck in the snow, shootings and I
wonder how many times they have reported forest fires with the
ranger station being closed October 1 through June 1. Everything
falls on them; without the phone, then what? And, would you believe
it, no mail service.*

*Alice walked the line one day last week, 8 miles up and back,
trying to find the break in the line. The wind is very damaging and
the timber cutters are very neglectful in letting trees fall against the
line, which, of course, puts it out of order. However, she did not find
the break. They themselves have fixed the line several times.*

*The nearest phone to them is Poudre Springs on the Little
South, six miles away. BUT one has to drive over Pennock Pass,
elevation 9,200 feet and the County does not keep it open, nor the
South Fork, during the winter months. Nearest phone to the east is
12 miles.*

*Jim Carson has delivered a 2-way radio to the Dickersons so
they do have a way to communicate with the outside world this
winter; that is five days a week which they are very thankful for.*

*Is there any way this phone line could be turned over to the
Dickersons?*

Jo Smethurst

"We wanted to buy the use of the telephone line, but they
wouldn't let us do that."

—Alice

12-15-76

Dear Alice and Helen:

*Mr. Carmack called me & said Mountain Bell has nothing to do
with the phone line—it is Forest Service responsibility and Carson
admits they have been lax on it. Mr. Carmack is sympathetic, but
says that in 1965 Mountain Bell approached you and the Forest
Service about putting in a line of their own to the two places and you
both turned them down. There has always been a hassle at the pole
where the Forest Service line connects onto the main Mountain Bell
Line of the South Fork, between the Forest Service and Mountain Bell.*

Jo Smethurst

"I said we could keep it up and the Forest Service said they
couldn't let us do that because somebody might get hurt and sue
the Forest Service. I said no, we wouldn't. We'd fix it up so we

could use it. But they fixed it up so we couldn't use it at all."
—Alice

3-2-77

Dear Mrs. Smethurst:
I have not forgotten about the Dickersons' telephone line. Members of my staff have been working with people on the Forest Supervisor's staff to consider the alternatives open to us. One of these is putting the line under permit to the Dickersons under the Granger-Thye Act. This would allow them to have it maintained at no cost to us. I can foresee 3 potential problems with this alternative: First, the cost may be prohibitive for the Dickersons; second, it may not be legal; and third, it still does not solve the safety problem I am concerned about with maintenance people working on the line.
James W. Carson
District Ranger

To Mr. Gunnar Jacobsen:
Your taking the time to write on behalf of the Dickersons is appreciated and I share your concern for their situation and welfare. For some time now I have been in contact with Forest Service officials in an effort to assist the Dickersons. The old Forest Service telephone line the Dickersons' telephone line is on is old, as you know, and the poles supporting the line are now rotted so that it is hazardous to maintain the line. Your kind offer to help maintain the line is truly generous, but neither Forest Service nor telephone company authorities would want anyone injured in caring for the telephone lines. Instead, the Forest Service has made arrangements to permit the Dickersons to keep the ranger's field radio at night. And I'm told they live very close to the ranger station for any help they might need during the day.
Jim Johnson
United States House of Representatives

"I said, give me my money back. We'd already put in enough money to pay for half a year. We got part of it back, at least."
—Alice

5-26-77

Dear Helen and Alice:
Since this is a Forest Service-owned line, Mountain Bell will not do anything to change the status of it without our permission; please direct your questions to me instead of John Cormack as there is no need for Mountain Bell to be involved until we contact them. We have checked our line out and it tested OK, so we had Mountain Bell

reconnect it; they said it still had problems. Please be assured we will do everything we can to get the line into operation as soon as possible.

James W. Carson
District Ranger

"A friend of mine, John Smethurst, and I were fixing the telephone line clear over to Pole #11 (a test pole) and the telephone company asked where we were calling from. That was past the Rockwell Ranch down toward the Poudre, through Jack's Gulch. They had a phone line to Pingree Park then. You could call from that pole to see if it was O.K. Then they fixed it so we couldn't call from there, either."

—Alice

5-26-77

Dear Mrs. Smethurst:
I see by your letter that your son fixed the line on May 18th. Although I appreciate his help and realize his good intentions, I'm afraid I must ask you to ask him not to work on the line. The line is a definite safety hazard, and the government could not be responsible for an accident.

I do not want Helen and Alice up there without communications.

James W. Carson
District Ranger

"We said in that case we'll just tear the telephone poles down (Helen and I) and cut them up for fence posts. I was getting one of them and I didn't know Helen was behind me and I gave it a flip and hit her leg and almost broke it. She had an ulcer on her leg for several years. I could have killed her; didn't even know she was there; might have hit her in the head. I picked up the insulators and gave them to different people and sold a few of them. I rolled up some of the telephone wire and used it for wreaths—at least I used it for something. We used the CB (like the Forest Service uses on their backpacks) Forest Service radios. We used those in the winter if they weren't using them, but in the summer we didn't have anything. They were the kind you had to take outdoors to call someone. The only people we could call was the Forest Service, and only during week days. When we wanted to get in touch with our neighbors, we couldn't. Only the Forest Service here or downtown."

—Alice

Dear Helen and Alice:

Our friend checked in Denver and he found out your phone is an extension of the Forest Service and when you are cut off it's because they do it so they can hear better on the phone and then they forget to turn you back on. Our friend is going to check with the Forest Service, but in the meantime you could remind that ranger station that they shouldn't leave your phone turned off.

Vera Metcalfe
Estes Park

10-19-78

Dear Mr. Oyler:

Gratitude to the Northern Amateur Communication Association of Larimer County for providing the sisters a 2-way radio. And Earl Morgan. Dickersons appreciate F.S. allowing them to use their frequency (Jim Carson & Henry Miller).

Jo Smethurst

1-29-79

(From Steamboat) It is nice to know that some of the things you do are appreciated and doubly nice when they take the time to say it. The Dickersons are grand ladies.

James W. Carson

MEMORANDUM OF UNDERSTANDING BETWEEN Northern Colorado Amateur Radio Club, Roosevelt National Forest and Helen and Alice Dickerson:

Provides for installation & maintenance of a VHF Radio supplied by NCARC and use on Roosevelt National Forest radio frequencies by the Dickersons, for official Forest Service business and emergency communications.

The Dickerson sisters maintain a residence near the Buckhorn Guard Station. Located in a remote area & no communication except Forest Service radio. Ranger station unmanned 6 months. Forest Service desires a degree of security afforded by occasional inspections on an unscheduled basis. Dickersons visit frequently but have no means of communication with the outside world except for occasional visits by friends. They were formerly under permit on a F.S. maintained telephone line now out of service and uneconomical to return to service. History of vandalism at station and breakins on Dickerson property. Numerous emergency situations, such as vehicle accidents and wildfires have been reported to Dickersons.

Used only for emergency or F.S or Sheriff matters. No personal or business interests by Dickersons.

Signed 3-1-79

"It was nice while it lasted."
—Alice

"Poor and content is rich and rich enough."
—Shakespeare

After all those years, there were many cheers
Echoing throughout the valley;
"The privy is out!" you could hear them all shout--
It sounded almost like a rally.
The ladies were aghast, it was done so fast
By Cecil and Roger and Irv;
They executed the flush without even a blush—
Oh, what comfort it would serve!

Alice finally gave up her '39 Chevrolet pickup she had for thirty nine years. She replaced that little jewel with a 1967 Chevrolet pickup with about 6000 miles spun under its chassis.

She kept it in her garage for three years and, except for Cecil Summers going up and driving it up the road a way once or twice a year, it just sat there. After three years, about 1983, Cecil took it to town and sold it for more than she had paid for it.

"It was getting so I was afraid to drive anymore; made me sick to drive a car. So Cecil and I decided I'd better get rid of it," said Alice, and dismissed the subject.

"All through the years they had no indoor bathroom," Cecil Summers recalled. *"The county finally ruled that Alice and Helen must either use a bucket under the seat or have a tank installed. So they put a bucket under and every morning you'd come up and see tracks in the snow where Alice carried it up over the hill and emptied it every day. We all decided it was time for these fine old ladies to enjoy one of the luxuries of life. So Roger Ellison, Irving Bartling and I in fall, 1984 got a septic tank and put it down below and across the road. We broke out the cement floor in their indoor bathroom and Irv installed the stool. Roger Ellison dug the ditch with his backhoe and we ran the sewer pipe across the road, down through the garden and into the septic tank down below. It was a great thing."*

And, in everyone else's opinion, they were great men.

Alice and Helen continued to do their crafts and people, mostly friends and acquaintances, of which there were many, stopped by the quaint log home to visit and buy. Helen's baskets were treasures to everyone, and she rarely had an extra one on hand; it was difficult to keep up with the demand. She was using at that time very long pine needles which she purchased from Louisiana. She found she could make the baskets much more

Alice with collage, Helen with baskets.   *Photo by Janet Robertson, 1988.*

Collage made by Alice. Photo by Alice, 1973.

214

quickly. Alice made collages, also in great demand, and little hummingbirds, and they, too, were not stockpiled.

"Pine needle baskets keep me pretty busy when I'm not working outdoors somewhere, like in the garden," Helen said. "We used to sell a lot of our potatoes, but in the last several years we haven't even raised what we could use."

Helen with their flower garden. Photo by Alice, early 1980s.

The telephone still hung on the wall. Silently.

"It actually helps since so many people tend to get stuck up this way at night," said Helen. "Now we don't have to decide whether to let strangers in to use the phone; we can just call to them without opening the door and tell them we don't have one."

They routinely fed the birds and squirrels every day without fail. Some birds and squirrels even became brazen enough to tap on the windows or doors if the sisters were a little tardy with the goodies. They cut down on the amounts of feed for humming-birds, however. "I just put one bottle out there and tell them, 'go eat a flower'," said Alice.

Helen coming in from the garden holding pansies with a flower in her mouth. Photo by Alice, 1981.

Cecil Summers said he was outside talking with Alice one day and they saw a coyote about 125 yards from them out in the meadow. Alice ran in, got her .410 shotgun, took aim and shot.

"You didn't get it, because there it goes into the trees," called Helen, who was watching from the kitchen window.

The next day Alice saw an unfamiliar lump out in the meadow. She walked over to it and there lay the coyote, dead. Cecil could not believe the shooting skill of Alice, the markswoman.

"I don't know if I hit it or scared it to death," she said. "Must have been two of the things."

Because of their vast array of good friends, the sisters had no need of a car. Friends brought the mail from the Masonville Post Office, food from Loveland or Ft. Collins and took them to town if it was necessary. Helen still did not like to leave home for any reason and Alice, her wanderlust subdued somewhat in her advanced years, did not care to leave much, either. Besides, they

Helen with pussywillows and chickadees.   *Photo by Alice 1983.*

Alice and pine squirrel.   *Photo by Patsey Bartling, 1983.*

leaned on each other at that time in their lives and neither one would have left the other alone unless absolutely necessary. They tried to repay those who ran errands, shoveled snow, sawed and chopped wood and fixed things by giving them crafts, homemade bread, a homecooked meal and always a little bit of kindness. Both sisters were acutely aware that "If they didn't help us, we wouldn't be able to stay. We really do appreciate their help."

Alice had no patience with people trying to get through deep, unplowed snow on Pennock Pass or Monument Gulch with ill-equipped vehicles, nor poachers, nor trespassers nor those who destroy other people's property. Because she, by nature, was so kind, she did not like to refuse help to anyone, but she was also well aware of the naivety of many young city people and keenly cognizant that some people could bring her harm.

One day some young people got stuck near her house. They came to her and asked for help. Alice told them, "If you do what I tell you, I'll get you out. You don't know what a deadman is I don't suppose. I'll get a piece of iron. Pound it into the ground at an angle, tie a cable on it and you can winch yourself out. Otherwise you'll stay here. They did it and they got out. They tried to pull the deadman out and they couldn't. It's still on the road for all I know. Long pipe with a sharp point on it. Tie a come-along to it and it works. I said, 'see? Now you kids get on home before it gets dark.'"

On October 6, 1980, a tragedy occurred on the Dickerson place. A young man, Jerry Chandler, loved the Dickerson ladies and enjoyed going up to their place so much, he called it his home. He had a falling out with his folks and brother, so he and a friend went up to see the ladies that fateful day. Instead of returning to Red Feather Lakes that night, they had decided to stay at the Dickersons'. Jerry went down to the meadow and tried to mount Earl Peterson's horse, which had "trespassed" into the meadow. Every time he tried to get on, the horse pawed at him. Alice, watching from the house, thought "that boy's going to get killed if he keeps that up." Then he went out of sight and she could hear him yelling and swearing up on the mountain. Then, silence. Jerry's friend went racing up there on his bike, only to return as fast as he could. Almost breathless, he yelled to Alice and Helen, "Jerry's dead!" The ladies felt just terrible, as did Earl, when he arrived. Earl could not believe his horse had killed the boy, but he got rid of it right away. No one knew what happened, but Jerry's skull was crushed.

Alice and Helen were invited to be Corn Roast Parade Marshalls in Loveland in 1989. Helen did not attend, but Alice went and thoroughly enjoyed the whole affair.

Alice. Grand Marshall, Corn Roast Parade, Loveland, August, 1989. Photo by Miriam Mohr.

Alice as Grand Marshall. Photo by Miriam Mohr, 1989.

LOVELAND
Corn Roast
"Nibble on my ear!"
Festival

September 9, 1989

Alice Dickerson
Box 10
Masonville, CO 80541

Dear Alice:

We would like to thank you for being the Corn Roast Parade Marshall this
year and helping to make it a huge success. We had so many nice comments
from the public about you and how pleased they were to get to see you and
how greatful they were that you came such a long way to be with us.

We hope that you enjoyed your day at the Corn Roast as much as we did.
Everyone always has such a good time and we hope you will be able to come
again next year.

Thank you again Alice, we love you.

Sincerely,

Dorothy + Harlene

Dorothy Rust
Harlene Cason
Co-Chairmen for Corn Roast Parade

Their garden was so beautiful people drove slowly by to
admire it and often stopped to take pictures.

The vegetables were bordered by spectacular displays of
flowers which added splashes of beautiful color to the mixed
greens of the vegetables, forest and meadow.

The Dickerson garden, June, 1993.   *Photo by Elyse Bliss.*

Alice still enjoyed fishing, although she no longer drove her car or walked too far away from the ranch.

Alice still enjoying
fishing, 1982.
Photo by Cecil Summers.

The ladies accepted each heavy snowstorm as a matter of course, although they knew life would be more difficult until it melted which, at that altitude, could be a long time.

Shoveling, bringing in wood and mopping up where melting snow seeped into the cellar were necessary chores to the Dickerson sisters and they executed them as routinely as most modern women load their automatic dishwashers. The big spring snow in 1983 provided them with some exercise at ages 74 and 75 but, as was their custom, they took it in their stride.

Helen carrying wood.
Photo by Alice, 1983.

Big snow.   *Photo by Alice, 1983.*

Helen feeding a chickadee in a 3' snow.
Photo by Alice, April 1983.

Alice and Helen both had serious hospital stays at different times and came home to recover.

Truly they were remarkable women.

VIII
THE UNIVERSITY OF
THE UPPER BUCKHORN
1992+

Cowbarn.

The Woodgatherers

With saw and axe they came in packs,
*   Felled and sawed quakies for the girls.*
Splitting it to size, they stacked to the skies;
*   They moved like tornado swirls.*
Food was abundant, but not redundant;
*   They ate 'til their stomachs swelled.*
Then sang many a tune by the light from the moon,
*   And vanished, their good deed upheld.*

Firewood gathering crew. Helen and Alice standing near center.
Photo by Dan Fink, September, 1987.

Probably the most impressive aid-the-Dickersons work force consisted of a varied assortment of mostly young people living in scattered locations along the Buckhorn Canyon. Each year, beginning in the 1980s, they got together on a September day and conducted their "wood party", which consisted of going up to the Dickerson ranch and cutting their winter wood supply. Summers, Ellisons, Sandmanns and others had been helping the sisters get in the wood supply in their later years, and now the young people pitched in to help. It was always a fun-filled day combining hard work and play. They cut, split and stacked the wood, ate a big pot luck picnic feast topped off by a songfest with multi-talented singers and musical instruments, many of which—dulcimers,

225

guitars, fiddles, banjos—were beautiful masterpieces constructed by local artisans. Posters were distributed, such as this message:

A Labor of Love for our friends !!!
The Third Annual
♥ Alice & Helen Dickerson ♥
Firewood Gathering Gathering
Sunday ~ September 2nd
9:00 a.m. 'til whatever it takes

We will be taking wood from their land this year so please show up with empty trucks and lots of ambition!

Please bring ~ trucks · chainsaws · axes · wedges · pot luck dish · musical instruments · firewood song

It was a day each year for the sisters to be grateful. All through the years they had sawed, split and carried down their wood for their winter supply. Now, they were well advanced in years and it was more difficult to do some of their age-old chores. The young people noticed and came frolicking to their aid. It became known simply as "the wood party."

Someone coined the title, "University of the Upper Buckhorn" for the Dickerson home and especially its inhabitants. Perhaps it was Marietta Neumeister; she wrote the article, "Bread on the Waters," in which she referred to it:

"The fall day was perfect for the Woodgathering Party at the Dickersons, high up in the Buckhorn Canyon, just short of Pennock Pass. The temperature was mild and the impossibly, blue Colorado sky accented the aspen, just beginning to turn gold.

"The Dickersons, often referred to as the sisters, Alice and Helen, the Dickerson girls and, most admiringly, as the University of the Upper Buckhorn, have lived there since first their family homesteaded the land in 1911.

226

Helen cutting wood. 1980s. Photo by Alice.

"Over the years, these unusual women have received many visitors for cookies and coffee in their kitchen. Each has thought to have discovered them and can't wait to tell of his discovery, only to find that they are well-known and not the recluses one might think. They have kept aware, through radio and their reading, of all that is happening in the world and there isn't a subject on which they can't comment. Those who have had the privilege of knowing them have found them to be caring women who are always ready to help others, even the stranger who must have the loan of a shovel to dig himself out of the snowdrift he has been warned about. Many a friend has benefited by the advice of these remarkable two.

"So, now, the tables are turning. As the Dickersons have gotten older, the many friends and acquaintances, yes, even the occasional visitor, have offered their help. One of the most festive occasions is the annual woodgathering in the fall, when people of all ages get together, at the Dickersons, to cut their supply of wood for the winter. I say festive because they all arrive with casseroles, desserts, salads, breads, as well as the necessary axes and saws. Some come with musical instruments made by the

artisans themselves. The hard work goes on all day, young and old, with good-humored teasing and much laughter. As the shadows lengthen, everyone crowds into the cabin to share their food with one another and crown the evening with music and song.

"Then, as they all make their way to their own homes, through the crisp, cool mountain air, they go with the feeling of work well done, that they have surely returned to the Dickersons, a measure of that which they have been given, so unstintingly over the years."

Woodcutting party, 1992.   *Photo by Sandy Glitch.*

Helen

Helen stayed home, not wanting to roam—
 Her home was the love of her life;
Her baskets were great, of Number One rate;
 She created them through good times or strife.
Riding horses she adored, didn't care for a Ford;
 She sold lots of crafts at her stand.
Her smile was a charm and her wit could disarm,
 And her kindness was best in the land.

Winter, 1991-92, was difficult for Alice and Helen, as well as for friends and relatives. Helen was gravely ill with cancer and her condition worsened as winter faded into spring. When Helen became so ill Alice could no longer take care of her, a friend took her to Poudre Valley Hospital in Fort Collins.

On April 1, 1992, Helen Esther Dickerson passed away and was buried in Fort Collins next to her parents.

The Buckhorn Newsletter of May, 1992, was dedicated to Alice and Helen:

"The 'girls', as they have always been affectionately called, were part and parcel of the Buckhorn Valley history. A slice of that history was eternally lost on April 1, 1992, when Helen Esther Dickerson passed away.

"At Helen's Commemoration Service, I made reference to the fact that she and Alice were craftsmen after the likes of those God chose to build the Tabernacle. The fine artistic work of Alice and Helen will live on for many years through their pine needle baskets and art work.

"To me the greater significance is the fact their extremely skilled and precise craftmanship will live on in the sanctuary of the Buckhorn Presbyterian Church. There is a stained glass window on the west side of the sanctuary. Mounted in the middle is a cedar cross, with the monogram IHS in the center. During Helen's service I mentioned that Alice and Helen crafted the cross and gave it to the church.

"So to both Helen and Alice we are grateful. They are part of the great number of God's special ones. We are thankful God placed them in the Buckhorn Valley."

—*Pastor Vic Urban.*

Helen Esther Dickerson. 1909-1992.   *Photo by Patsey Bartling, 1983.*

Now Alice was alone.

Alaska

She saw grizzly bears fresh out of their lairs,
Shaggy muskoxen and tiny infant moose,
Sea otters and whales and caribou males,
Bald eagles in air and on roost.
Denali was bright, it was dazzling white;
She walked on a glacier near its top.
She panned for gold, caught halibut in the cold
And hated for the adventure to stop.

Alice remained on the homestead after her sister passed away.

It was time to plant the garden, so friends helped her plow; then she planted, as was her custom, her potatoes, carrots and other vegetables.

Having been friends of the sisters, Elyse Bliss, thinking Alice might like to see Alaska, invited her to accompany her on a business trip. She said that would be fine. So away they went, on a longer trip than Elyse had anticipated, because she knew Alice would want to see as much as possible of her first love, wildlife. It was raining when they left, so she knew that, at least on her first of eighteen days away from home, her garden would be watered.

Elyse wrote a synopsis of their Alaskan adventure in the July, 1992 POUDRE PROFILE, entitled,"Alice's Adventures in Wonderland". All photos are by Elyse Bliss. The article:

Five years ago POUDRE PROFILE featured a story, "Our Ladies of the Mountains," about Helen and Alice Dickerson. For over 80 years the pioneer ladies have been living legends in these parts.

When people who knew Alice expressed shock and disbelief about Alice going to Alaska or anywhere else for that matter, Alice answered,

"I went to Ohio once on a Greyhound bus."

"When was that, Alice?"

"About 50 years ago. It was before the war."

May 23rd we commenced Alice's adventure in the far north. This is a synopsis of that journey by our pioneer lady of the Rockies who to this day lights her log cabin by gaslight and bakes grand-champion-quality homemade bread in a wood stove.

The turbulence halfway to Anchorage from Seattle that changed a smooth flight to a slightly bumpy one prompted Alice to display

a touch of nervousness. She turned away from the window in the United 737 and, with obvious concern expressed in her eyes, asked,

"Will this thing turn upside down?"

Assuring her that it was unlikely, I calmly explained turbulence as best I could, concealing my white knuckles under the snack tray.

She relaxed, then, and returned her gaze out the window to the Alaskan coastal waters near Juneau far below. But she still didn't like those wiggling wings, and said so.

Descending toward Anchorage, I pointed out familiar landmarks to her as the big aircraft approached the runway—Chugach Mountains, Cook Inlet, the stunted scrawny Alaskan Black Spruce trees. We were about to touch down on Alaskan soil...the first time Alice Dickerson had seen the ocean or flown in a plane as she seldom ventures out of her mountain habitat.

Suddenly the aircraft pulled up sharply instead of touching down on Alaskan turf as promised. I grabbed the headphones and heard a controller say to our pilot the approach was too high: "bank to the right and execute a lower approach."

The concerned look reappeared in Alice's eyes.

"Why didn't we land?"

"He came in too high," I explained, "and he has to do it over again, only lower."

"For heaven's sake. Hasn't he been here before?" she commented and returned to her porthole.

This time he made a perfect landing and we were in Alaska.

Immediately we drove in our rented car to the Kenai Peninsula. Alice loves wildlife and even claims to be one of them herself, so at Cooper's Landing we stopped to "glass" the mountains and spied several Dall sheep and a mountain goat...all prominent white dots on the green slope, in contrast to our Rocky

Mountain Bighorn sheep, which blend into the vegetation. Alice counted them...5, 6, then 9...a pair of ewes with lambs, so casually, you would think she was in a zoo. She enjoyed the turquoise Kenai River and at Kenai she glimpsed cloud-shrouded Mt. Redoubt, an active volcano in its majestic white setting across Cook Inlet. Arriving at my friends' North Kenai lakeside home, we heard loons calling on the lake.

We sat glued listening to Joe and Betty Cloud tell us about their upcoming gold-mining venture on Alaska's North Slope. Then, feeling tired, we began becoming accustomed to the long Alaskan summer daylight; it was midnight there and we had arisen at 4:45 a.m. in Colorado. We spent Alice's first "night" in Alaska needing no flashlight and the loons still calling hauntingly in the late dusklike night.

For the next 17 days we trekked through the Land of the Midnight Sun, stopping at will to view and take pictures of wildlife and scenery.

At Homer, first chance she got, Alice scooped up some salt

Snap

water "just to see what it tastes like."

Alice tasting saltwater.

By the time we went halibut fishing in Kachemak Bay, Alice was becoming a seasoned sailor. She caught more than her limit and had to return some to the sea. The Captain of the Lucky Pierre invited her to the cabin to take the wheel, which she did calmly and admirably. Later, when returning, an engine blew and we crippled into the Homer Spit on "a wing and a prayer."

Alice halibut fishing.

Alice's first-ever train ride was a short, two-tunnel excursion on an Alaska Railroad train to Whittier.

Our sea excursions ranged from the large Alaska ferry, "T u s t e m e n a", across Kachemak Bay to Seldovia, to smaller cruise boats that slipped between shorelines of fjords in the beautiful waters of Resurrection Bay, Kenai Fjords National Park and Prince William Sound. Wildlife was

*Alice on the
Tustemena*

abundant—seabirds, sea otters, whales, sea lions and seals.

*Alice touching the
pipeline.*

Enjoying unlimited mileage, we cruised into the great Alaska Interior, stopping to see every moose and caribou alongside the road,

234

the Muskox Farm in Palmer, the oil pipeline, Valdez and its pipeline terminal, a fishwheel in the Copper River at Chitina, miles and miles of beautiful scenery on the old Denali Highway between Paxson and Cantwell and it never did get dark!

Alice and the helicopter pilot.

We flew in a helicopter over Denali Park, Alice calmly snapping pictures from her side window of the spectacular scenery below. An hour later we were speeding up the Nenana River in a jet boat at breakneck speed to spend the evening at a working gold mine and trapper's camp. Alice panned for gold and shook down some real flakes.

Alice panning for gold

Two dazzling clear days hosted us in Denali Park. Grizzly bears, ptarmigan, Dall sheep, fox, caribou, moose and awesome Mt. Denali gleaming white against a blue sky thrilled us as we drove leisurely to Kantishna Lodge at the very end of the park.

The evening after leaving Denali Park we boarded a small plane at Talkeetna and flew onto Mt. Denali (McKinley), our continent's highest mountain, landing on skis on Ruth Glacier. We cruised through pinnacles so near the wingtips that Alice said if we'd had a gust of wind, we would have been history. While walking on the glacier the air felt like it was 80°. It was the most spectacular sight I've ever seen and, standing atop 3000' of ice, Alice called it "magnificent". It was a perfect ending to three weeks of fun-packed adventure and Alice plucked up a chunk of glacier ice and brought it home in a bottle.

Elyse and Alice, Ruth Glacier on Mount McKinley.   Photo by pilot.

We returned our car, 2500+ miles older, and Alice returned to her cabin under the Colorado sky.

An Alaskan's assessment of our lady of the mountains: "She's like a real sourdough*; you would think she'd lived in Alaska all her life." I call her a walking encyclopedia and just knowing her is an education in itself. She has retained it all from the old days and frosted that with today's vast information.

Alice assesses her adventure in the Alaskan Wonderland: "It's the most fun I've ever had in my life; we did it all."

*"Sourdough" means seasoned Alaskan; "Cheechako" is a newcomer.

Teton Country

Teton country in the West is beauty at its best;
   Yellowstone showed burns reduced to coals.
Elk bugled loud, grizzlies scared the crowd,
   Buffalo stood too close to geyser holes.
Presidents' faces at night, bright in the brilliant light;
   Mammoth bones in prehistoric muds.
Ferrets in their dens, couldn't get them in the lens,
   Alice went home, pulled her carrots and dug her spuds.

Alice (left) waiting for raft to be unloaded for a float trip on the Snake River, Grand Teton National Park, 1992.   Photo by Elyse Bliss.

After she returned from her exhilarating trip to the Land of the Midnight Sun, Alice spent the summer of 1992 at home. She took care of her garden, entertained visitors by the droves, created little pine-cone hummingbirds and watched, on her solar-powered TV, nature and other educational programs on Denver's Channel 6. Jack Greer having retired, Charles Bliss, of Poudre Canyon, harvested her hay in August.

Following the wood party in September Alice and Elyse went

Cow elk cooling their heels.   *Photo by Elyse Bliss.*

to Grand Teton and Yellowstone National Parks, timing the trip so she could watch and hear the elk during rutting season. Not only did she see and hear vast numbers of elk, but they were privileged to observe two grizzly bears for several hours in Yellowstone. They drove up into Montana so Alice could see Custer's Battlefield after driving over the Bighorn Mountains in Wyoming. They saw Devils Tower, Dakota Badlands National Park and Mt. Rushmore before arriving at the spot

Alice, Devil's Tower, Wyoming, 1992. Photo by Elyse Bliss.

where archaeologists and volunteers were excavating the big pile of ancient mammoths. It was difficult getting Alice out of there. After visiting Fort Laramie, they traversed westerly to the Wyoming Division of Wildlife Research Station where the biologists were working with the near-extinct black-footed ferrets, before returning home.

*   *   *   *   *

Alice, at age 84, went out into her beautiful garden and harvested her vegetables, including potatoes and carrots, and stored them in the cellar for her winter food.

Dickerson home and garden.

When she had finished her other age-old end-of-fall chores, she was ready for the long, cold winter, her 81st on the homestead.

Alice at her stove, 1993.   *Photo by Elyse Bliss.*

Cranes and Kings

Thousands of cranes, in spite of spring rains
  Came cruising down from the skies
Which blackened when they came, these cranes of fame—
  Alice couldn't believe her eyes!
Then she flew back, Alaska map in her pack
  To the Land of the Midnight Sun.
She hooked a large king & they heard her sing,
  "A great big salmon, this one!"

Three of Alice's friends, Jane Wallower, Miriam Mohr and Marge Schneider took Alice to Kearney, Nebraska in the spring of 1993 so she could watch the annual northward migration of thousands of sandhill cranes, snow geese and other avian species. Alice returned excited, rejuvenated and full of enthusiasm for the thrilling sights and sounds of the birds on the move.

Sandhill Cranes in Nebraska.   *Photo by Miriam Mohr, Spring, 1993*

Apparently not wanting to be left behind by the northward-bound birds, Alice answered her own call of the wild. With her Alaska travel companion repeating as guide, Alice returned to Alaska and saw some new Alaskan country and different wildlife, including Kodiak bears. She again fished for halibut and again succeeded, but she was even more thrilled to hook a seventeen pound king salmon on the Kenai River.

Boat captain and Alice with her salmon. Kenai River, Alaska, 1993.
Photo by Elyse Bliss.

Back home again, once more she tended her summer garden and stood ready to go wherever her friends would take her—to see what she could see.

Alice.   Photo by Sandy Glitch, 1992.

Sure enough. In the fall she rode a train from Laramie, Wyoming to Fox Park, Colorado with friends Nancy Oyster and Jay Arrasmith to view the beautiful fall colors. Then she and Elyse whipped up to Canada's High Arctic ... to see the polar bears.

She snapped picture after picture of every bear she saw ... almost.

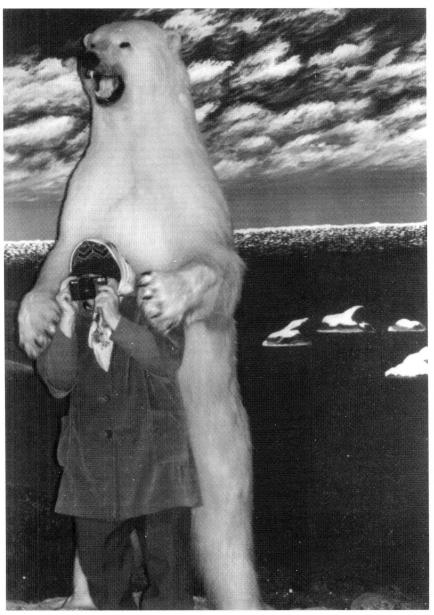

"Hurry, Alice ... point and shoot!" Photo by Elyse Bliss. Churchill,
Manitoba,Canada, October 1993.

Apples of the Mummy's Eye

The horse barn's gone and the other looks wan--
Worn by the stresses of time;
The sawmill's erased and the soddy can't be traced;
Phantoms of a past so sublime.
Their cabin may go but we all will know
That Alice and Helen won't die.
The Range o'er the pass will ensure they will last;
They're the apples of the Mummy's eye.

All knowledge does not come from high schools or the formal universities. The revered Dickerson sisters did not only survive wilderness living for the better part of a century, but mastered living in harmony with the harsh environment that became as natural to them as migration for birds, hibernation for bears and seasonal rejuvenation of leaves.

Roland G. Parvin, ex-chairman of the Colorado Game and Fish Department, now Colorado Division of Wildlife, said in 1924,

"Our lives have become so artificial that the saving influence of the out-of-doors is needed to counteract the confinements of city life. We need to live more among the forest and mountains to re-establish the ancient kinship between the race and nature....."

Perhaps his statement explains at least partly the Dickerson sisters' phenomenon.

Alice, had she had the opportunity, could have been a university professor of biology, botany, zoology or ornithology. She had a remarkable memory and an insatiable curiosity even as a small child, when she drove her grandfather "nuts" with her unending questions.

It was not just their mastery of living with the harsh elements that brought admiration from all who met them, but their insight into and acceptance of all people, their "live and let live" attitude (except for wrong-doers), their gentleness, generosity and kindness, lack of worship of the almighty dollar and their reluctance to board the speeding train of our fast-paced world. The past is alive within the walls of their practical little cabin. Its lone inhabitant moves about so methodically that any observer can readily discern that she has dwelled there a long time. Friends are with her almost constantly now...to keep her safe by night and day. Grooved into the old linoleum on the floor between the kitchen and (indoor) shed is an unmistakable trail made by two or three sets of feet over an extended period of time.

Time-worn trails on linoleum in Dickerson home.
Photo by Elyse Bliss, 1993.

The Dickerson sisters were true diligent remnants of the best of our past, and entering their world gave one the feeling that time had stood still; yet, curiously, it had not; nor had they.

* *

The Mummy Range lies silently with all its lofty peaks towering above the world below. Within range of its imaginary vision the little Dickerson homestead has remained intact for over 80 years. On that homestead lived two five foot tall little girls who have always been and always will be the apples of the Mummy's eye.

The Mummy Range.   *Photo by Alan Dakan, late 30s.*

Apples of the Mummy's Eye: Alice and Helen Dickerson.
Photo by Jimbo Wilson, 1980.

SUGGESTED FURTHER READING
AND SOURCES

Articles About the Dickerson Sisters
"Bread on the Waters." Publication unknown.
   Marietta Neumeister.
"Close to Home." Sue Lenthe, August 19-20, 1989, *Loveland Daily Reporter-Herald*.
"The Dickersons: Our Ladies of the Mountains." Elyse Bliss, July, 1987. *Poudre Profile*.
"Helen's Death Leaves a Void on Buckhorn." Earle Wilson. April 30, 1992, *Fort Collins Triangle Review*.
"Historical Notes of the Buckhorn Canyon and Surrounding Areas," by Helen and Alice Dickerson, 1977-78.
"Living Legends." Dan MacArthur, Nov. 14, 1991 *Fort Collins Triangle Review.*
"The Mountains: A Refuge." The Magnificent Mountain Women, Adventures in the Colorado Rockies, Alice & Helen Dickerson, pp. 185-186. Janet Robertson. 1990. University of Nebraska, Lincoln, NE. 220 pp.
"Pioneer of Buckhorn Canyon Dies at 82." Terrie Alto, April 2, 1992, *Fort Collins Coloradoan*, p. 1.
"Primitive Lifestyle Suits Dickerson Sisters Just Fine." Sally McGrath.*Loveland Daily Reporter-Herald*, August,1982.p.16.
"Sisters in 70s Work as a Team." Patricia Gallagher. *Fort Collins Coloradoan*, July 11, 1984.
"Sisters Live in Old 'Mountain Tradition'" by Mildred Camp. *Loveland Daily Reporter-Herald*, Valley Homemaker Section,Loveland, CO. September 26, 1973.
"So You Think You Were Snowbound." *The Fence Post*, Jan. 10, 1983.
"The Undaunted Dickersons." Red Fenwick, 1954. *The Denver Post*.
"When They Stop and Smell the Roses." Andrea Galliher. *The Fence Post*, Feb. 22, 1988. pp 4-6.
Other Sources
Earth Roads. Maurice O. Eldridge. *Farmers' Bulletin 136*, 1902. U. S. Department of Agriculture.
Farm Storage of Apples and Potatoes. James L. McGinnis, Colorado Office of Markets, Denver, CO, Colorado Agricultural College Extension Service, Fort Collins, CO. *Extension Bulletin, Series 1, #121*. August, 1917.

Grasshopper Control. Charles R. Jones. *Bulletin 233*, 1917. The Agricultural Experiment Station of the Colorado Agricultural College, Fort Collins, Colorado.

"Introducing a New/Old Alternative to Cedar Shake Roofs." Sue Lenthe, *The Trading Post*, March 11-17, 1982, p. 16.

"Old Fire Tower Finding New Life in Local Park." Francis Clark, *Fort Collins Triangle Review*, May, 1987.

Books

Cache La Poudre "The River" as seen from 1889. Norman Walter Fry. Second printing.

Colorado. A Bicentennial History. Marshall Sprague. 1976. W.W. Norton & Company, Inc. New York, NY. 204pp.

Colorado Front Range: A Landscape Divided. Gleaves Whitney. Johnson Publishing Company, Boulder, CO. c. 1983.

Colorado Mountain Ranges No. 2. Jeff Rennicke. Falcon Press. Colorado Geographic Series, #2. c. 1986. Helena and Billings, Montana.

Colorado Skylines. Front Range from the East. Book 1. Robert M. Ormes. Bound by American Bindery, Topeka, Kansas.

Colorado's Wildlife Story. Pete Barrows and Judith Holmes. 1990. Colorado Division of Wildlife.

Compilation of the Messages and Papers of the Presidents. A. Joint Committee of Printing in the House and Senate pursuant to an Act of the 52nd Congress of the United States. 1913. Published by the Bureau of National Literature.Vol IX.Index.

Farm Machinery and Farm Motors. J. Brownlee Davidson and Leon Wilson Chase. 1916. Orange Judd Company, New York and London. 513pp.

Guide to the Colorado Mountains. Robert Ormes with the Colorado Mountain Club. Swallow Press, Inc. Chicago, 6th Edition, 5th Printing, 1974.

History of Masonville School, A. Morning Glories Extension Homemakers Club of Larimer County, Colorado. 1986. Osborne Publishing Co., Inc., Osborne, KS. 204pp.

Life of Birds, The. Joel Carl Welty, W.B. Saunders Co., 1962.

Rocky Mountain Mammals, by David M. Armstrong. Rocky Mountain Nature Association, Inc., 1975.

Rocky Mountain National Park Hiking Trails—Including Indian Peaks. Kent and Donna Dannen. 1978. East Woods Press Books. 287pp.

<u>Wild Mammals of Colorado: Their Appearance, Habits, Distribu-</u>
<u>tion and Abundance</u>, by R.R. Lechleitner. Pruett Publishing
Co. Boulder,CO 80302, 1969.